Study Guide and Mapping Workbook for

World Regional Geography

by Lydia Mihelic Pulsipher and Alex Pulsipher

Fifth Edition

◊ Jennifer Rogalsky

State University of New York, College at Geneseo

◊ Helen Ruth Aspaas

Virginia Commonwealth University

W.H. Freeman and Company

New York

EXECUTIVE EDITOR: STEVEN RIGOLOSI

MARKETING MANAGER: JOHN BRITCH

SUPPLEMENTS EDITOR: KERRI RUSSINI

ISBN-10: 1-4292-5349-5

ISBN-13: 978-1-4292-5349-9

PRINTED IN THE UNITED STATES OF AMERICA

FIRST PRINTING

W.H. FREEMAN AND COMPANY

41 MADISON AVENUE

NEW YORK, NY 10010

HOUNDMILLS, BASINGSTOKE R621 6XS, ENGLAND

WWW.WHFREEMAN.COM/GEOGRAPHY

Contents

Preface

This workbook and study guide is designed to accompany the fifth edition of Lydia Pulsipher and Alex Pulsipher's *World Regional Geography*. The questions and exercises contain references to relevant tables, figures, and photo essays that appear in the fifth edition.

Each chapter of this workbook begins with **Learning Objectives** and **Key Terms**. These sections are intended for reference and for review of the main ideas of each chapter.

Your instructor may choose to use the **Review Questions** for class discussion or ask you to turn in written answers. You may decide to read through these questions before you read the textbook as guides to the main concepts in the textbook. These questions may also be used to review for an exam. Keep in mind that these questions cover only some of the material discussed in the textbook; they do not refer to every point made.

The **Critical Thinking Exercises** ask you to apply the concepts discussed in the textbook. These exercises may ask you to perform a task based on your daily routine, browse the Internet, or consider how your life might be different if you lived in another country. These exercises are designed to be stimulating and entertaining, while helping you to understand important geographic concepts.

Because places are so important in geography, a list of **Important Places** is provided for each region; most countries, capital cities, significant physical features, and other places discussed in the textbook are listed. You are asked to locate these places, and to note important facts about them.

It is likely that your instructor will ask you to turn in the **Mapping Exercises** as assignments. These exercises will help you understand and explain geographic patterns. You are given blank maps to complete each exercise, and blank world maps for context. You can download additional copies of the maps from the textbook's Web site: www.whfreeman.com/pulsipher5e.

Finally, **Sample Exam Questions** are given for each chapter to test your knowledge of information and understanding of concepts from the textbook.

We hope you enjoy working through this student workbook. It should challenge and stimulate you to read the textbook thoroughly; it should also be fun, as you apply these situations to your own life and attempt to understand the complex geographic patterns and relationships of the world in which we live.

Enjoy!

JENNIFER ROGALSKY AND HELEN RUTH ASPAAS

Media Guide for Students

Textbook Companion Site
www.whfreeman.com/pulsipher5e

For each of the 11 chapters in the textbook, the textbook companion site serves as an online study guide, offering:

Map Learning Exercises: Students can use these exercises to identify and learn about the countries, cities, and major geographic features of each region.

Map Builder and Map Builder Exercises: Chapter-by-chapter Flash programs allow students and instructors to create their own thematic maps. A simple interface allows users to choose the data to place together on a single map, which can then be printed. The zoom feature of this Flash program provides detailed views of any area of the custom map. *A Guide to Using Map Builder* is included as a .pdf file, and a specific Map Builder exercise is provided for each chapter of the textbook.

Thinking Critically about Geography: This feature encourages critical reflections on the global linkages of trade, finance, tourism, and political movements. The activities in this section allow students to explore how a geographic perspective helps clarify our understanding of such issues as democratization and conflict ("War and Peace"), water provision and rights ("Water, Water, Everywhere"), and global climate change. A number of links to a variety of Web sites that students can explore are included; these are matched with questions or brief activities that give students an opportunity to think about the ways their lives are connected to the places and people they read about in the textbook. *Thinking Critically about Geography* helps students focus on key concepts, such as scale, region, place, and interaction, by using these concepts to drive analysis of compelling issues.

Blank Outline Maps: Printable maps of every world region are provided for note-taking or exam review.

Online Quizzing: A self-quizzing feature enables students to review key textbook concepts and sharpen their ability to analyze geographic material for exam preparation. Two quizzes are provided for each chapter. The first quiz focuses on key concepts; the second is specific to subregions.

Flashcards: A set of matching exercises helps students learn vocabulary and definitions for each chapter in the textbook.

Audio Pronunciation Guide: A spoken guide for the pronunciation of place names, regional terms, and geographic vocabulary is provided.

World Recipes and Cuisines (from *International Home Cooking*, the United Nations International School Cookbook): Class exercises and social events can be organized around the use of these recipes, through which students can gain an awareness and appreciation for international cuisine.

Selected Readings and *Web Links*: Additional suggestions for further reading in each chapter are provided.

CHAPTER ONE
Geography: An Exploration of Connections

LEARNING OBJECTIVES

In each chapter of the textbook, nine common themes help to provide a basis for understanding regional information and for making comparisons among regions. The nine themes are climate change, democratization, development, food, gender, globalization, population, urbanization, and water. The learning objectives for each chapter focus on these nine common themes.

After reading the chapter and working through this study guide, you should understand how the textbook's nine thematic concepts relate to world regions.

- Climate change: Know how humans are impacting climate and how some countries are attempting to reduce their impact. Also understand that those who are causing climate change are not always those experiencing the worst effects.
- Democratization: Understand the importance of political issues in geography, including civil society, geopolitics, and international cooperation. Also understand why democracy is expanding in the world.
- Development: Know how human well-being can be measured and how these measures differ. Also understand the concept of sustainable development as it relates to food, the environment, economics, culture, and human well-being.
- Food: Understand how food systems can keep pace with population growth. Also understand the risks associated with various methods of increasing food supply.
- Gender: Understand that gender roles differ across regions and cultures and that these roles significantly affect how a society works. Also understand why gender roles differ among places and how they are changing.
- Globalization: Know what it means to be part of the global economy. Understand that globalization is a dynamic process that has differential effects on rich and poor countries.
- Population: Know how and why patterns of population growth and density differ from region to region. Understand some of the effects these patterns may have on gender and wealth.
- Urbanization: Understand the reasons that cities are growing, but also understand that conditions are not always as good as migrants expect when they arrive in cities.
- Water: Understand where and why pressures are increasing on water supplies, and know that some modern technologies may be able to help with water quality and distribution.

KEY TERMS

The following terms are in **bold** in the textbook. Page numbers for each term can be found in the Chapter Key Terms list at the end of the textbook chapter. In the space next to the term (or on a separate sheet or flash cards), you can fill in the definitions for reference or quiz yourself for exam review. Definitions are found in the glossary of the textbook, as well as in the sidebars on the page they first appear.

agriculture

authoritarianism

biosphere

birth rate

capitalism

carrying capacity

cash economy

civil society

climate

climate change

communism

culture

death rate

delta

democratization

demographic transition

development

domestication

ecological footprint

erosion

ethnic cleansing

ethnic group

fair trade

female earned income as a percent of male earned income (F/MEI)

floodplain

food security

formal economy

free trade

gender

gender roles

genetic modification (GM)

genocide

Geographic Information Science (GIS)

geopolitics

global economy

global scale

global warming

globalization

green revolution

greenhouse gases

gross domestic product (GDP)

gross domestic product (GDP) per capita PPP

human geography

human well-being

informal economy

interregional linkage

Kyoto Protocol

landforms

lines of latitude

lines of longitude

living wages

local scale

map projections

material culture

migration

monsoon

multiculturalism

multinational corporations

Neolithic Revolution

nongovernmental organization (NGO)

orographic rainfall

physical geography

plate tectonics

political ecologist

population pyramid

purchasing power parity (PPP)

push/pull phenomenon of urbanization

race

rate of natural increase (RNI)

region

Ring of Fire

scale (of a map)

sex

slums

subregions

subsistence economy

sustainable agriculture

sustainable development

total fertility rate (TFR)

United Nations (UN)

United Nations Human Development Index (HDI)

urbanization

virtual water

water footprint

weathering

world region

World Trade Organization (WTO)

REVIEW QUESTIONS

The following review questions are related directly to the textbook material. These questions can be used to help you prepare for an exam, or you may want to read through the questions before you begin reading the textbook, quizzing yourself after you complete each section.

Introduction
1. What is the study of geography? How are maps used as tools for analysis?
2. List at least three challenges that geographers encounter as they designate the regions of the world.

Population
3. Relate the J curve to the growth of human populations over the last 2000 years. Why and where is population growing?
4. If you observe a population pyramid for a country that shows fewer girls and women than boys and men, what conclusions can you draw about that country's gender issues? Name at least two other dynamic processes you can infer about a country from its population pyramid.

Gender
5. Although activities assigned to men and women differ among cultures and eras, what are some of the consistencies? Attempt to explain the situations in which education levels or income levels are higher for females than for males.

Development
6. Identify the pros and cons of using each of the following as a development measure: gross domestic product per capita, United Nations Human Development Index, and female earned income as a percent of male income. Suggest a situation that can lead to a country having a low GDP per capita but a high HDI and F/MEI.
7. Why is sustainable development important, and how can it be achieved in a world of economic development, increasing standards of living, and increased rural-to-urban migration?

Food
8. How have changes in agricultural production over the past 150 years impacted the supply and security of food, and how have they altered the environment? Are the green revolution and genetic modification the solutions to food-supply and environmental problems?

Urbanization
9. Why are cities growing, and what pattern of growth is most common for cities in the developing world? What conditions prevail in many developing world cities?

Globalization

10. Identify at least three potential impacts of the arrival of a multinational manufacturing or assembly plant in a highly traditional culture. What are the risks and opportunities associated with this connection to globalization?

11. How can workers who live in one country earn relatively high wages when compared to workers in another country, yet still live in poverty?

Democratization

12. Where and why is democracy growing and spreading? What factors are helping, and what factors are hindering democratization?

Water

13. What do you think is the biggest problem with water: usage, access, or quality? Explain your choice and why you didn't choose the other two options.

Climate Change

14. What is being done to diminish the impact that humans are having on the environment? What more can be done? Why is the relatively rich minority of the world's population causing such problems for the environment? How is this pattern changing as the developing countries industrialize, modernize, and urbanize?

Physical Geography Perspectives

15. How can you account for Africa's general plateau-like surface?

16. Fully explain the process that creates monsoons. Include a discussion of temperature and air pressure, as well as differential heating and cooling of water.

Human Geography Perspectives

17. Explain the tie between trade and the domestication of plants.

18. What is the difference between culture and ethnicity? How is culture changing with technology and globalization?

19. How is language related to culture? What is happening to the diversity of languages, and what effect will this have on cultures in the future? Why has English evolved as the global lingua franca?

20. Although race is not seen as biologically significant, why does it have political and social importance?

CRITICAL THINKING EXERCISES

The following questions ask you to apply the ideas and principles you learned from the textbook to new situations.

1. Geography and its relations to other disciplines

Geography can be defined as the study of our planet's surface and the processes that shape it. However, geographers usually specialize in one or more fields of study.

- Consider your academic field of interest. How does it fit into geography?
- In what ways does your field of interest fit into one of the geography subdisciplines listed in the "What is Geography?" section of your textbook?
- If you are not a geographer by training, in what ways could a geographic perspective *add to* the study in your own academic discipline?

2. Formal and informal economies

The formal economy includes all the activities that are recorded as part of a country's official production. The informal economy, however, includes goods and services that are produced outside formal markets, often for no cash or for payment that is not reported to the government.

- Consider the type of "informal economy" employment you have had in the last five years. Why was this work *not* part of the formal economy?
- What are/were the positive effects of this on your life and the lives of others?
- What are/were the negative effects of this on your life and the lives of others?
- Because of educational, racial, or gender restrictions, imagine that you were able to *only* be part of the informal economy. How would this affect the quality of your life in the past, present, and future?
- What would your life be like if you could not do any work in the informal economy?

3. The future of urban conditions

The world's population is now half urban, large cities are becoming more numerous, and the size of cities is ever larger.

- How would you define "urban," meaning what characteristics do you think need to be present for a place to be considered urban?
- Would you like to live in an urban area? If so, what location and kinds of opportunities would you prefer? If not, why not?
- View the introductory video at http://theplaceswelive.com and then choose at least one of the four locations on the world map to view the conditions in which the family lives. Compare this to the conditions in the city nearest to where you live.
- What do you think is the future of urban areas? What do you think needs to be done in light of the fact that cities are becoming larger, and more and more people are migrating to them from rural areas?

4. Pacific Ring of Fire

The Pacific Ring of Fire is an especially active area of volcanoes and earthquakes. In recent years, it has received worldwide attention, as hundreds of thousands of people have died because of tectonic activity (and the resulting tsunamis, earthquakes, and volcanoes).

- Examine Figure 1.21 (Ring of Fire), which includes locations of earthquakes, volcanoes, and plate boundaries.
- Visit earthquake.usgs.gov/regional/world/historical_country.php for a list of recent earthquakes. Click on the hyperlinks to view maps and read about the events.
- Open *Google Earth* and turn on the volcanoes layer. Browse through some of the posted photos, Web sites, and news articles to see images of, and read about, recent volcano eruptions.
- Using the Internet, find the Banda Aceh region and the epicenter of the 2004 Indian Ocean tsunami: www.noaanews.noaa.gov/stories2004/s2357.htm. Also visit the following sites to view animations and maps:
  - www.intute.ac.uk/sciences/hazards/images/tsunami_2004_full.gif
  - www.cbc.ca/news/background/asia_earthquake/gfx/map_epicentre.jpg
  - Finally, use the Internet to search for before and after images of the tsunami-affected areas.
- Reflect on what you've seen on these Web sites. What would life be like if you lived in the Ring of Fire? What methods could you use to adapt and cope with these potentially life-threatening events?

5. Values and ways of knowing

All cultures establish, preserve, and pass on knowledge, which is grounded in a set of values. These values and norms differ from culture to culture (and sometimes within cultures); thus, a type of behavior might be admired by some but reviled by others.

- Select a non-Western cultural group that is represented on your campus. Ask a member of that group to identify some of his or her culture's values (e.g., role of the parents in family life, rules about dating, who takes care of the elders, etc.).
- Identify similarities between your culture's values and those of the non-Western culture. Identify differences.
- Suggest a generalization about why there are similarities but distinguishing differences between Western cultures and non-Western cultures.
- Are there overarching values or standards among cultures?
- How can we be sensitive to differences among places and within cultures regarding larger issues of human rights (oppression, genocide, torture, etc.) without accepting inhumane behavior?

MAPPING EXERCISES

The following mapping exercises are designed to improve your knowledge of the location of places, underscore why they are important, and clarify how they relate to one another. Some questions will ask you to locate places, compare maps, or fill in data; others will test your understanding of *why* you were asked to map the features that you did. Use the blank outline maps at the end of the chapter to complete these exercises. See Appendix B for blank outline maps of the World. Additional blank outline maps can be found on the textbook's Web site: www.whfreeman.com/pulsipher5e.

1. Differences and complementarity among HDI, GDP, and gender equity

Human well-being is difficult to define and to measure. However, if we look at several measures together, we can better understand the subtleties and nuances of well-being.

- Carefully examine the three global maps of human well-being (Figure 1.15).

Questions

   a. What are the benefits of using more than one variable to assess human well-being?
   b. What relationship(s) do you expect among the three variables (GDP per capita, HDI rank, and F/MEI). Explain your answer(s).
   c. Pick out three countries that are anomalies (e.g., high GDP but low HDI rank; or high HDI and low F/MEI) and attempt to explain what could cause these discrepancies.

2. Arable land, agriculture, and soil degradation

Soil erosion appears to be an environmental concern in many countries, but it may be more serious in those countries where the economy has a high dependency on agriculture. All the countries in South Asia are facing soil degradation issues.

- Visit the CIA World Factbook at www.cia.gov/library/publications/the-world-factbook/index.html.
- Collect information on percent of arable land, percent of population who earn their living from agriculture, and the GDP per capita for the countries of South Asia: India, Pakistan, Bangladesh, Afghanistan, Nepal, Bhutan, Sri Lanka, and the Maldives.
- Select appropriate symbols to map these three sets of information on the blank map of South Asia. You may want to use shading for one variable, cross-hatching for another variable, and a symbol of your choice for the third variable.

Questions

   a. From the map you created and the map of development and deforestation (Photo Essay 1.2), identify at least three challenges that farmers face if they want to slow the rate of soil degradation occurring on their farms.
   b. Identify the country that may have the most serious challenges in arresting soil degradation, and explain why you selected that particular country.

c. Examine the map of undernourishment in the world (Figure 1.16) and discuss the potential impacts on nutrition of environmental degradation.

d. Examine the map of GDP per capita (Figure 1.15) and discuss how, as a region, South Asia can manage such environmental problems with such limited GDP per capita.

3. Climate classifications

Climate, wind, and weather are largely the result of complex patterns of air temperature and pressure, ocean temperature and currents, and the location of certain landforms.

<u>Questions</u>

a. Consider the climate of where you currently live. List the general climate characteristics including temperature, precipitation, and seasonality characteristics.

b. Next look at Photo Essay 1.6 (climate regions). Write down the classification that corresponds to your area.

c. If the classification matches how you described your area, attempt to explain your climate characteristics. If the description or classification does not match yours well, explain why it does not match. Consider the scale of the map in the photo essay, as well as any mountain ranges or bodies of water that may affect climate.

SAMPLE EXAM QUESTIONS

The following are sample questions to help you review for an exam. Answers are found in the back of this study guide.

1. Which of the following terms refers to the study of how people, objects, or ideas are, or are not, related to one another across space?
a) regional geography
b) physical geography
c) cartography
d) spatial analysis

2. Death rates remained high for most of human history for all of the following reasons except:
a) hygienic waste and sewage systems
b) fluctuating food availability
c) disease
d) natural disasters and hazards

3. Which of the following is NOT a positive "ripple effect" of developing countries investing more resources in the education of females?
a) Educated women are more likely to migrate to another country.
b) The children of educated women are more likely to finish secondary school.
c) The children of educated women are healthier.
d) Educated women have fewer children, which helps the family financially.

4. Developing nations are usually characterized by _____ economies, while developed nations are usually characterized by the presence of _____ industries.
a) agricultural, service
b) industrial, service
c) service, agricultural
d) industrial, knowledge-based

5. At the global level, which of the following best explains the fact that around one-fifth of the world's human population subsists on insufficient and inadequate diets?
a) Extra food is produced but does not often get to those who need it.
b) Rapid population growth has outstripped increases in world food production.
c) Environmental degradation has curtailed increases in world food production.
d) World food production is insufficient due to the inefficiencies of socialism.

6. All of the following cities are home to the "new" middle class of educated urban residents, except for:
a) Cape Town, South Africa
b) Mumbai, India
c) Shanghai, China
d) Mexico City, Mexico

7. What is the key goal of multinational corporations?
a) the development of world trade
b) environmental protection
c) increased employment in host countries
d) profit

8. Which of the following statements about the United Nations is true?
a) It focuses on the development of socialist-type economies.
b) It possesses its own standing army that is larger than any other except China's.
c) Its rulings pertaining to nation-states are not legally binding.
d) It consists of all developed countries except those from the former Soviet bloc.

9. Water scarcity is the result of all of the following except:
a) population growth
b) increased per capita demand for water due to modernization
c) inequitable allocation of water
d) sustainable farming initiatives

10. About 70% of the carbon dioxide (CO_2) in the atmosphere comes from _____; the remainder comes from _____.
a) animal flatulence; the use of fossil fuels
b) photosynthesis; animal flatulence
c) the use of fossil fuels; the loss of trees and other forest organisms
d) evaporated water pollutants; agricultural fertilizers

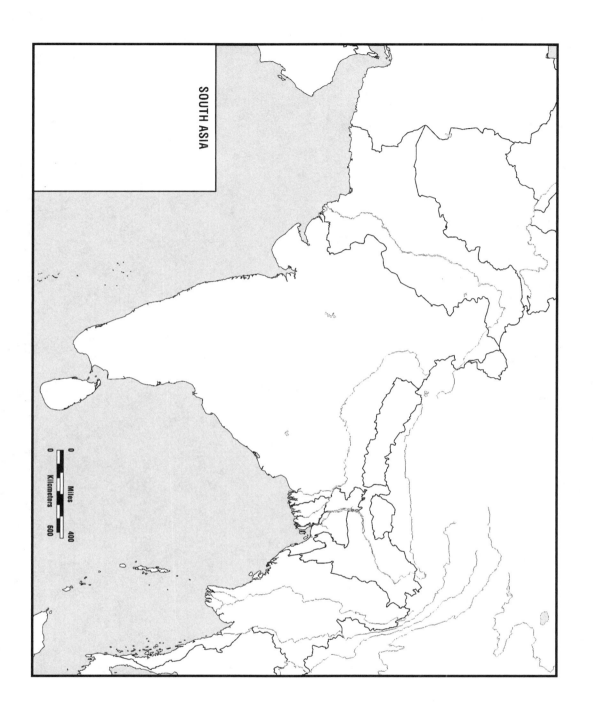

SOUTH ASIA

0 Miles 400
0 Kilometers 600

CHAPTER TWO
North America

LEARNING OBJECTIVES

After reading the chapter and working through this study guide, you should understand how the textbook's nine thematic concepts relate to North America.

- Climate change: Understand how the economic vitality and standard of living for this region has affected the environment and resulted in environmental degradation that has global ramifications.
- Democratization: Understand how issues of national security associated with war and immigration are testing perceptions of individual rights and national safety.
- Development: This region ranks first in terms of wealth and productivity, yet disparities exist. Be able to identify spatial, ethnic and gender disparities and how they are being resolved.
- Food: North America is comprised of two large countries whose diverse and complex landforms are often associated with a variety of climatic patterns that in turn affect settlement patterns and agricultural practices. In this context, understand the important transitions that are occurring in agriculture and how these impacts are part of a larger economic transition away from industry to postindustrial service and technology economies.
- Gender: Understand that women are attaining career opportunities based on completion of high levels of education. Be able to identify the challenges they face in terms of income disparity between themselves and their male counterparts.
- Globalization: Be able to identify some of the social, political, economic, and environmental interactions between this region and the rest of the world and be able to characterize challenges that arise in forging such relations.
- Population: Historical and contemporary processes transform the population densities and the ethnic diversity of North America. Be able to explain how mobility and a well-educated workforce are related to the growth of post industrial livelihoods.
- Urbanization: The population of North America is highly urbanized. Be able to identify the negative impacts of urban sprawl on the environment.
- Water: Identify the influence of large bodies of water on regional climates. Explain how this influence results in various agricultural responses. Understand the growing dependency on water to produce crops and the conflict that arises over the best use of this water for burgeoning urban populations.

KEY TERMS

The following terms are in **bold** in the textbook. Page numbers for each term can be found in the Chapter Key Terms list at the end of the textbook chapter. In the space next to the term (or on a separate sheet or flash cards), you can fill in the definitions for reference or quiz yourself for exam review. Definitions are found in the glossary of the textbook, as well as in the sidebars on the page they first appear.

acid rain

agribusiness

aquifers

brownfields

clear-cutting

digital divide

economic core

ethnicity

genetically modified organisms (GMOs)

gentrification

Hispanic

information technology (IT)

infrastructure

megalopolis

metropolitan areas

North American Free Trade Agreement (NAFTA)

nuclear family

Pacific Rim

Québecois

service sector

social safety net

suburbs

trade deficit

tundra (Subregions textbook version only)

urban sprawl

REVIEW QUESTIONS

The following review questions are related directly to the textbook material. These questions can be used to help you prepare for an exam, or you may want to read through the questions before you begin reading the textbook, quizzing yourself after you complete each section.

The Geographic Setting

1. What are the geologic processes responsible for the physical landscape of the three major landforms: the Rocky Mountains, the Appalachian Mountains, and the Central Lowlands?
2. Winds, mountain ranges, and water bodies account for prevailing weather conditions and climatic patterns in much of North America. What are the general impacts of each of the major water bodies on regional weather conditions?
3. Water is relatively abundant in this region, yet we see much concern for its safe and careful use. List three water-related themes from this chapter and identify problematic issues associated with the three themes you selected.
4. The North American lifestyle is associated with serious environmental degradation. What human-related activities have profoundly affected the loss of habitat for plants and animals and/or led to wide scale land, water or air pollution?
5. Name five key events that have affected the ethnic and geographic redistribution of population in this region. What factors led to the population shift from northeastern United States to the Southeast and the West?

Current Geographic Issues

6. Name at least two divisive issues associated with the increasing focus on national security within the United States. Explain the reasons for these debates.
7. Name two criteria that suggest that Canada's dependency on the United States is much greater than the dependency of the United States on Canada. Explain how Canada is able to maintain its autonomy, despite having a powerful neighbor along its southern border.

8. What major changes have taken place in the methods of agricultural production during the past 100 years? How do these changes affect the relationship between agriculture and national economies, employment, and markets? What are the impacts of these changes on the consumer, both domestically and internationally?

9. Compare agriculture, manufacturing, and services to each other in terms of share of the economy and percent of labor force involvement. Relate your findings to existing human resources in the region.

10. How has this region used global connections to further its economic interests? What are the chief challenges faced by this region when engaging in the globalized economy?

11. What is the role of the social safety net in light of the 2008 global economic downturn? How does the social safety net vary between the United States and Canada?

12. Despite increased opportunities for women in North America, many aspects of men's and women's lives are not at parity. What are some of these differences? How can we account for differences between Canada and the United States?

13. What are three problematic processes associated with urbanization? Explain programs and policies enacted to alleviate these problems.

14. How do immigrants take from and contribute back to their communities and economies? How do such activities relate to the current debate on limiting immigration to the United States?

15. What are some arguments that may help explain persistent poverty in this region? How do single-parent households and spatial segregation based on class relate to these arguments?

16. What factors led to the evolution of the nuclear family? What factors appear to be influencing its demise in the twenty-first century?

17. Explain why some regions are gaining large populations and other regions are losing population. How do mobility and aging play a role in these notable regional population shifts?

18. As the percent of the aging population in North America increases, new forms of residential life are emerging. Identify at least two of the options mentioned in the textbook and provide a corresponding rationale for these alternate forms of residential life.

19. What factors have promoted a high incidence of mobility among this region's population? What are some long-term impacts on the social fabric of the region?

20. Explain why the maps that depict GDP and HDI are misleading about the overall patterns of human well-being in this region.

CRITICAL THINKING EXERCISES

The following questions ask you to apply the ideas and principles you learned from the textbook to new situations.

1. Hispanic influences on American culture

Hispanics comprise the principal source of immigration into the United States. Figure 2.21 (changing national origins of legal U.S. immigrants) and Figure 2.23 (changing U.S. ethnic population) give visual evidence of the immigration of Hispanics into North America.

- Make at least three observations regarding the impact of an increased Hispanic population presence on American culture and lifestyles today. For example, some sources suggest that salsa has replaced ketchup as the condiment of choice on the average American table.
- How have some of your personal activities and preferences changed as a result of this influence?
- Suggest three impacts that might result from continued immigration of Hispanics into the United States during the next decade or two. If your impacts imply a problematic situation, then suggest means of alleviating them.
- What are some of the most strident arguments against immigration that you have heard around campus or in your community? Likewise, what are some of the most supportive arguments favoring immigration that you have heard recently?
- After examining these two sides of the debate, reach some form of consensus that balances both perspectives.

2. Americans and their food

The textbook authors present two quite divergent perspectives about agriculture in North America. One segment focuses on the "family farm" and the second discusses the rise of corporate agriculture. Using the concepts of "spin-offs" and "multiplier effects" that are presented on page 82, discuss the following:

- What are the "spin-offs" and "multiplier effects" that come from the family farm?
- What are the "spin-offs" and "multiplier effects" that come from corporate agriculture?
- Identify at least three ways in which your own food purchases and dining habits contribute to the family farm and/or corporate agriculture?
- What if the family farm were to disappear. How would such an event affect your eating habits and your understanding about sources of your food?
- What if corporate agriculture were deemed illegal? How would the end of corporate farming affect your eating habits and your understanding about sources of your food?

3. Changing family structures in North America

The family structure in North America experienced considerable change during the last half of the twentieth century. This change continues into the twenty-first century.

- Examine your own family's structure as it exists today and compare it to that of your parents when they were growing up, and also to that of your grandparents when they were children. You may be fortunate enough to be able to evaluate the family structure of your great-grandparents.
- Using these case studies, determine if your family structure for the past three (or four) generations matches the changes over time in American family structure as discussed in the text.
- Examine Figure 2.26 (U.S. households by type) and relate your family structure to this figure.

4. Aging: Different perspectives from different generations

Different generations may respond to issues associated with aging in different ways. As the aging population of North America increases, some long-held perspectives about the aging are undergoing revision.

- If possible, ask your parents and grandparents what their expectations were of "old age" when they were in college or just beginning their careers. Ask your parents and grandparents how their expectations of "old age" and retirement have changed as they have aged.
- What are your own expectations of "old age" now?
- Compare your perceptions of aging to that of your parents, and if possible to that of your grandparents.
- Compare and contrast your findings to the discussion in the textbook about aging in North America.
- While population growth increases environmental impacts, slower population growth increases the population that is elderly, leaving fewer young working people to shoulder the demands of a growing economy. In light of this, should population growth be curtailed?
  - Place the justification for slower growth against the need for young workers in North America and provide some workable solutions.

5. Mobility and suburbia in North America

One principal characteristic of the North American population is the frequency with which it moves about. Many of these moves are to the suburbs, despite growing concerns about urban sprawl and loss of valuable agricultural land.

- Reflect on your own experiences with moving both as you were growing up and as you entered college. Describe the rationale for each of those moves.
- How does your own history of mobility compare to that discussed in the chapter?
- What perceptions of both the central city and the suburbs do people in the United States and Canada have that encourage the movement to suburbia? What local, state, and federal policies *encourage* the move to suburbia?

- What benefits are accrued to society by enhancing urban areas and retarding the rush to the suburbs? Generate at least three of your own ideas that could entice suburban residents back to the cities?

IMPORTANT PLACES

The following places are featured in the chapter. Make sure you can locate all of them on a map. Blank outline maps can be found on the textbook's Web site: www.whfreeman.com/pulsipher5e. Also, to prepare for quizzes and exams, write a few important facts about each place in the space provided.

Physical Features

1.   Appalachian Mountains

2.   Atlantic Ocean

3.   Bering Strait

4.   Catskill Mountains

5.   Colorado River

6.   Grand Banks

7.   Great Basin

8.   Great Lakes

9.   Great Plains

10.   Gulf of Mexico

11.   Mississippi River drainage basin

12.   Mississippi Delta

13.   Newfoundland Island

14.   Ogallala Aquifer

15.   Ohio River

16.   Pacific Ocean

17.   Rocky Mountains

18.   Sacramento River

19.   San Francisco Bay

20.   San Joaquin River

21.   Utah Valley

Regions/Countries/States/Provinces

22.   Alabama

23.   Alaska

24.   Alberta

25.   Arizona

26.   Arctic

27.   Arkansas

28.   California

29.   Canada

30.   Carolinas (The)

31.   central lowland

32.   Central Valley, CA

33.   Colorado

34.   Connecticut

35.   Dakotas (The)

36.   Dogrib Territory

37.   Dust Bowl

38.   Florida

39.   Georgia

40.   Great Plains

41.   Gulf Coast

42.   Idaho

43.   Illinois

44.   Iowa

45.   Kansas

46.   Kentucky

47.   Louisiana

48.   Maine

49.   Manitoba

50.   Maryland

51.   Massachusetts

52.   mid-Atlantic economic core (old economic core)

53.   Middle West

54.   Minnesota

55.   Mississippi

56.   Missouri

57.   Mountain West

58.   Nebraska

59.   Nevada

60.   New Brunswick

61.   New England

62. Newfoundland

63. New Jersey

64. New Mexico

65. New York

66. North Dakota

67. Northeast

68. Nunavut Territory

69. Oklahoma

70. Olympic Peninsula

71. Oregon

72. Pacific Coast

73. Pacific Northwest

74. Pennsylvania

75. Québec

76. Rhode Island

77. Saskatchewan

78. San Francisco Bay Area

79. South Carolina

80. South Dakota

81. Southeast (the American South)

82. Southwest

83. Tennessee

84. Texas

85.   United States of America

86.   Utah

87.   Virginia

88.   Washington

89.   West (the American West)

90.   West Coast

91.   Wisconsin

Cities/Urban Areas

92.   Atlanta, GA

93.   Baltimore, MD

94.   Barrow, AK

95.   Boston, MA

96.   Cairo, IL

97.   Cambridge, Ontario

98.   Charlotte, NC

99.   Chicago, IL

100.   Cleveland, OH

101.   Dallas, TX

102.   Detroit, MI

103.   Eugene, OR

104.   Gainesville, FL

105.   Georgetown, KY

106.   Homestead, PA

107. Ipswich, MA

108. Kingston, TN

109. Knoxville, TN

110. Los Angeles, CA

111. Lowell, MA

112. Memphis, TN

113. Milwaukee, WI

114. New York, NY

115. Ottawa, Ontario

116. Philadelphia, PA

117. Phoenix, AZ

118. Pittsburgh, PA

119. Pittsford, NY

120. Portland, OR

121. Princeton, IN

122. Providence, RI

123. Rochester, NY

124. San Diego, CA

125. San Francisco, CA

126. Seattle, WA

127. St. Louis, MO

128. Terrebone Parish, LA

129. Valdez, AL

130.   Vancouver, British Columbia

131.   Washington, D.C.

132.   West Point, GA

133.   Woodstock, Ontario

MAPPING EXERCISES

The following mapping exercises are designed to improve your knowledge of the location of places, underscore why they are important, and clarify how they relate to one another. In these exercises, you will not do any mapping, but you will carefully interpret textbook maps in order to draw some conclusions. A blank map of North America is provided at the end of this chapter for reference.

1. Regional climate, population density, and agriculture practices

Agriculture in North America is highly productive, but usually in areas with favorable climates and abundant natural resources.
- Use the climate map (Photo Essay 2.1), the population density map (Photo Essay 2.6), and the agriculture map (Figure 2.15) to answer the following questions.

Questions
   a.   What are two possible human and two physical geography explanations for the location of the *mixed farming* activities?
   b.   What are two possible human and two physical geography explanations for the location of the *range livestock* activities?
   c.   What are two possible human and two physical geography explanations for the location of *corn belt, cash grain*, and *livestock* activities?

2. Mobility and aging in developed societies

For a multitude of reasons, the populations of this region are highly mobile. In some cases, mobility can increase as one ages, especially for those eager to enjoy the amenities of warm climates, say, in Arizona or Florida.
- Use the population by region map (Figure 2.28) and the changing distribution of elderly map (Figure 2.30) to answer the following questions.

Questions
   a.   Which regions of the United States have experienced the largest increase in population between the years of 1900 and 2000? Provide at least three reasons to explain this noteworthy redistribution of the U.S. population.
   b.   It was noted previously that Arizona and Florida attract many senior citizens who move to these states to enjoy retirement. How, then, do we explain the growing population of elderly in the Great Plains Breadbasket, the Rust Belt, and New England?

3. Environmental issues in North America

North America's environmental issues vary across the region. Some issues are highly localized while others affect large populations.

- Use the air and water pollution map (Figure 2.4), the population density map (Photo Essay 2.6), the agriculture map (Figure 2.15), and the human impact map (Photo Essay 2.2) to answer the following questions.

<u>Questions</u>

    a. Which environmental issues are likely to be associated with high population densities? Why is this the case?

    b. Which environmental issues are not likely to be associated with high population densities? Why is this the case?

SAMPLE EXAM QUESTIONS

The following are sample questions to help you review for an exam. Answers are found in the back of this study guide.

1. Which term does the text use to refer to all Spanish-speaking people from Middle and South America?
a) Latino
b) Hispanic
c) South American
d) Hispaniola

2. The Great Lakes were formed by:
a) plate tectonics.
b) melting glaciers.
c) global warming.
d) the Appalachian mountains.

3. What process resulted in the formation of the North American central lowland that lies between the two major mountain ranges of the continent?
a) A colossal volcanic eruption split North America in half, and the central lowland, once an intercontinental sea, was filled in by glacial activity.
b) Earthquakes opened and flattened what was once a mountainous area.
c) Material that erodes from the Rocky Mountains has been deposited by wind, rain, and rivers.
d) Early European settlers cleared and flattened a hilly landscape so that they could more easily farm the area.

4. A climate that is dry and warm in summer, cool and moist in winter is:
a) Mediterranean.
b) Tyrrhenian.
c) American.
d) Pacific.

5. Which of the following is not an environmental challenge facing North America?
a) continental cooling
b) depletion and pollution of water resources
c) habitat loss
d) hazardous waste

6. A particularly strong threat to the North American environment comes from the burning of _____ to generate electricity.
a) natural gas
b) coal
c) lumber
d) paper

7. In the United States, a disproportionate amount of hazardous waste is disposed of in locations inhabited by:
a) suburbanites.
b) deer and other wildlife.
c) poor people and minorities.
d) those of European heritage.

8. The vibrant agricultural economy of central and southern California was made possible mostly by government-funded:
a) immigration.
b) irrigation.
c) oil pipelines.
d) farm subsidies.

9. Which of the following is true regarding the U.S. and Canadian economies?
a) The United States is more dependent on Canada than vice versa.
b) Canada is more dependent on the United States than vice versa.
c) Both trade more with Japan than each other.
d) Both trade more with Europe than each other.

10. The passage of the North American Free Trade Act (NAFTA) has had which of the following effects?
a) considerable decline in trade between the United States and Canada
b) reduction and removal of tariffs among Mexico, the United States, and Canada
c) rising corruption in Canada due to United States' and Mexican firms who have relocated there
d) sharp decline in the flow of Mexican migrants into North America

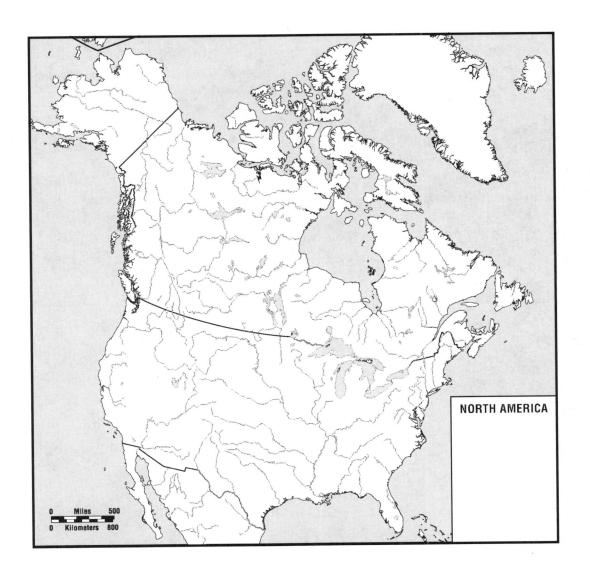

NORTH AMERICA

0 Miles 500
0 Kilometers 800

North America   33

CHAPTER THREE
Middle and South America

LEARNING OBJECTIVES

After reading the chapter and working through this study guide, you should understand how the textbook's nine thematic concepts relate to Middle and South America.

- Climate change: Know basic landform and climate patterns, including the tectonic forces in the region and how climate varies across the large land and island landmass. Understand why this region is vulnerable to climate change and how people are adapting to change.
- Democratization: Understand why democracy is still so fragile in this region and what can be done to make it succeed.
- Development: Understand the influence of colonization on the landscape, settlement patterns, economy, and populations of countries in the region. Understand why inequities still exist across the region.
- Food: Understand why the region is shifting toward large-scale agriculture and how this results in conflict over space.
- Gender: Understand the importance of family life, especially the extended family. Understand the importance and consequences of *machismo* and *marianismo*.
- Globalization: Know the causes and effects of structural adjustment programs, the overwhelming debt that many countries are facing, and free trade agreements in this region.
- Population: Understand the general patterns of population distribution. Know why some countries are still growing rapidly while others are growing quite slowly.
- Urbanization: Understand the push and pull factors that result in rural-to-urban migration. Understand the effects this large influx of people has on cities in the region.
- Water: Know the environmental issues that are threatening ecosystems in this region. Understand how economic development and the environment are linked.

KEY TERMS

The following terms are in **bold** in the textbook. Page numbers for each term can be found in the Chapter Key Terms list at the end of the textbook chapter. In the space next to the term (or on a separate sheet or flash cards), you can fill in the definitions for reference or quiz yourself for exam review. Definitions are found in the glossary of the textbook, as well as in the sidebars on the page they first appear.

acculturation

Altiplano (Subregions textbook version only)

assimilation

Aztecs

biodiversity

brain drain

commodification

contested space

coup d'état

Creoles

dictator

early extractive phase

ecotourism

El Niño

evangelical Protestantism

Export Processing Zones (EPZs)

extended family

external debts

fair trade movement

favelas

foreign direct investment (FDI)

forward capital (Subregions textbook version only)

haciendas

import substitution industrialization (ISI)

Incas

income disparity

indigenous

isthmus (Subregions textbook version only)

ladino (Subregions textbook version only)

land reform

liberation theology

machismo

maquiladoras

marianismo

marketization

mercantilism

Mercosur

mestizos

Middle America

(to) nationalize

North American Free Trade Agreement (NAFTA)

plantation

populist movements

primate city

privatization

recession

shifting cultivation

silt

South America

structural adjustment policies (SAPs)

subduction zone

temperature-altitude zones

trade winds

urban growth poles (Subregions textbook version only)

World Trade Organization (WTO)

REVIEW QUESTIONS

The following review questions are related directly to the textbook material. These questions can be used to help you prepare for an exam, or you may want to read through the questions before you begin reading the textbook, quizzing yourself after you complete each section.

The Geographic Setting
1. How do plate tectonics affect physical geography in this region?
2. Explain why this region has such climatic diversity.
3. What are some of the known effects of El Niño and hurricanes on this region?

4. Many are concerned about the fast pace of rain forest loss. What are some human activities that result in deforestation? What are some effects of deforestation and climate change in this region?
5. Why is ecotourism an appealing development idea for some countries in this region? What may be some of the drawbacks?
6. What were the strengths of the Aztecs and Incas during the conquest? How did the Spanish defeat them, given the relatively small number of Spanish soldiers?
7. What is the basic relationship between a mother country and its colonies in Middle and South America? In what ways were both the populations of the mother countries and the colonies affected by colonization?

Current Geographic Issues
8. Give a brief description of the three stages of economic development as presented in the textbook. Include information on the type of industry common in each stage, the impact of government intervention, and the effects on the economy and population.
9. If a country has an import substitution policy, what kinds of things do you think it may try to manufacture? What are the advantages and disadvantages?
10. Why has it been determined that structural adjustment programs (SAPs) will help with national debt? What are the impacts of the SAPs and current debt at the personal, regional, and national levels?
11. What factors have led to widespread participation in the informal economy? What are the positive and negative outcomes on individuals and economies?
12. What are the positive and negative impacts of free trade agreements at the personal, regional, and national levels?
13. How is contested space related to inequities, and how do conflicts vary at different scales (local, provincial, national, and world)?
14. Many factors can compromise the success of establishing and maintaining a democracy. What are some obstacles to stability and democracy in Middle and South America?
15. What are the positive and negative consequences of population growth? Why do some countries have such high rates of natural increase, while others are quite low? What does rapid growth mean for economies and human well-being?
16. What circumstances could explain why gross domestic product (GDP) per capita might be relatively low for a country, yet its Human Development Index (HDI) rank might be high? What factors form the basis for saying that the quality of life is relatively high in the Caribbean?
17. What are some differences between extended families and nuclear families? How does an extended family affect the arrangement of living space, relationships between parents and children, and spending of family income?
18. What are the roles, reasons for, and effects of *machismo* and *marianismo*? What transitions are occurring in both of these roles in the twenty-first century?

19. What are some of the reasons for rural-to-urban migration? What are some of the outcomes in both the origin (rural villages) and the destination (cities)? Understand what city life is like in favelas. Understand what city life is like for a woman in this region.
20. Explain how liberation theology, populist movements, and evangelical Protestantism address the matter of wealth and poverty in quite different ways.

CRITICAL THINKING EXERCISES

The following questions ask you to apply the ideas and principles you learned from the textbook to new situations.

1. Participation in the formal economy

By examining the transitions associated with NAFTA and other trade agreements in the region, we know that many people are taking jobs in the formal sector, leaving their livelihoods in the informal sector behind.

- List new areas of employment in which people in the region are participating (e.g., maquiladoras and the tourism industry).
- What may be the positive effects of this transition on one's life, as well as their family?
- What may be the negative effects of this transition on one's life, as well as their family?
- What might life be like in this region if people could only work in the formal economy?

2. Measures of human well-being

GDP ignores certain aspects of well-being that HDI and F/EIM take into account. Each measure, however, does give us important information about a place. Much can be revealed when we look at all three measures in one country.

- Using the maps of human well-being (Figure 3.18), choose a country in this region that has data for all three variables.
- Using the textbook *and* the library or Internet (start with the CIA World Factbook: www.cia.gov/cia/publications/factbook), research this country and attempt to explain what factors contribute to each of these three index values.
- Discuss any measures that seem to contradict each other (or are significantly different).

3. Extended families

Extended families are very important and are the basic social institution in all societies in Middle and South America.

- What are some of the benefits of an extended family in this region? How does it affect daily life?

- Do you have an extended family? Do they live nearby or even in the same house? Why do you think this is so?
- What do you think the positive and negative effects of an extended family are or would be in your life?

4. Are *machismo* and *marianismo* present in your society?

Gender roles in Middle and South America are based heavily on the concepts of *machismo* and *marianismo*.

- Outline the characteristics and roles associated with each *machismo* and *marianismo*.
- What are the pros and cons of the roles of *machismo* and *marianismo*? Consider their effects on both males and females.
- Do you see similar roles in the society in which you live? How are they similar and different? Why is this the case?
- Describe any changes you foresee in gender roles in the years to come in your society.
- How would changes such as these affect the development of Middle and South America?

5. Migration push and pull factors

Migration is one of the most important social forces in the world today. Many economic and social factors initiate and sustain migration, and likewise it has many social and economic effects.

- Consider where you live or attend college now. What are the reasons you left the last place you lived (push factors)?
- Have you ever had to move because of something beyond your control, like drought (as did the couple in the vignette about Fortaleza, Brazil)? If so, what was this like; if not, what would this be like?
- What factors drew you to the place where you live now (pull factors)? Did you have to worry about whether there would be enough jobs, housing, and services, like many people do in Middle and South America?
- What ties do you still have to the place you once lived? Has your decision to live where you are now influenced any others to migrate to your location?
- Do you plan to move away from your current location, perhaps after graduation? If so, what are the push and pull factors that will influence your move?

IMPORTANT PLACES

The following places are featured in the chapter. Make sure you can locate all of them on a map. Blank outline maps can be found on the textbook's Web site: www.whfreeman.com/pulsipher5e. Also, to prepare for quizzes and exams, write a few important facts about each place in the space provided.

Physical Features

1.   Altiplano

2.   Amazon Basin

3.   Amazon River

4.   Andes Mountains

5.   Atacama Desert

6.   Atlantic Ocean

7.   Baja California

8.   Brazilian Highlands

9.   Caribbean Sea

10.   Greater Antilles

11.   Guiana Highlands

12.   Gulf of California

13.   Gulf of Mexico

14.   Gulf of Panama

15.   Hispaniola

16.   Lake Titicaca

17.   Lesser Antilles

18.   Llanos

19. Mato Grosso

20. Orinoco River

21. Pacific Ocean

22. Pampas

23. Parana River

24. Patagonia

25. Rio Grande River

26. Sierra Madre Occidental

27. Sierra Madre Oriental

28. Tierra del Fuego

29. Yucatan Peninsula

Regions/Countries/States/Provinces

30. Anguilla

31. Antigua & Barbuda

32. Argentina

33. Bahamas

34. Barbados

35. Belize

36. Bolivia

37. Brazil

38. British Virgin Islands

39. Chile

40. Colombia

41. Costa Rica

42. Cuba

43. Dominica

44. Dominican Republic

45. Ecuador

46. El Salvador

47. Falkland Islands

48. French Guiana

49. Gálapagos Islands

50. Grenada

51. Guadaloupe

52. Guatemala

53. Guyana

54. Haiti

55. Honduras

56. Jamaica

57. Martinique

58. Mexico

59. Montserrat

60. Nicaragua

61. Panama

62.   Paraguay

63.   Peru

64.   Puerto Rico

65.   St. Kitts & Nevis

66.   St. Lucia

67.   St. Martin

68.   St. Vincent & the Grenadines

69.   Suriname

70.   Trinidad & Tobago

71.   Uruguay

72.   Venezuela

73.   Virgin Islands

Cities/Urban Areas

74.   Asunción

75.   Belmopan

76.   Bogotá

77.   Brasília

78.   Buenos Aires

79.   Caracas

80.   Cayenne

81.   Chiapas

82.   Fortaleza

83.   Georgetown

84.   Guatemala City

85.   Havana

86.   Kingston

87.   La Paz

88.   Lima

89.   Managua

90.   Mexico City

91.   Montevideo

92.   Panama City

93.   Paramaribo

94.   Port-au-Prince

95.   Port of Spain

96.   Quito

97.   Rio de Janeiro

98.   San José

99.   San Juan

100. San Salvador

101. Santiago

102. Santo Domingo

103. Sucre

MAPPING EXERCISES

The following mapping exercises are designed to improve your knowledge of the location of places, underscore why they are important, and clarify how they relate to one another. Some questions will ask you to locate places, compare maps, or fill in data; others will test your understanding of *why* you were asked to map the features that you did. Use the blank outline maps at the end of the chapter to complete these exercises. Additional blank outline maps can be found on the textbook's Web site: www.whfreeman.com/pulsipher5e.

1. Landforms, the environment, and population density

The region of Middle and South America extends south from the midlatitudes of the Northern Hemisphere, across the equator, nearly to Antarctica. Within this vast expanse, there is a wide variety of highland and lowland landforms; some landforms are more conducive to human settlement than others.

- Draw the general outline and label the following landforms from the regional map of Middle and South America (Figure 3.1): Sierra Madre Occidental, Sierra Madre Oriental, Guiana Highlands, Andes Mountains, Brazilian Highlands, Atacama Desert, and Patagonia.
- Also, trace the Amazon River with a thick blue line, and draw the outline of the Amazon Basin with a lighter blue line.
- Using the map of population density (Photo Essay 3.5), shade the areas (in red) that have more than 261 people per square mile (more than 100 people per square kilometer).

Questions
  a. Analyzing your map, describe the general spatial distribution of population.
  b. Explain why some highland areas have high population concentrations. Explain why some highland areas have low population concentrations.
  c. Explain why some lowland areas have high population concentrations. Explain why some lowland areas have low population concentrations.

2. International drug trade

The international drug trade can lead to corruption, violence, and subversion of democracy in the region.

- Shade the GDP per capita for each country in the region (Figure 3.18), using the following categories: $0-1999; $2000-9999; and $10,000 or greater.
- Using Figure 3.15 (Interregional linkages: cocaine), use a graduated symbol (much like the one presented on the map in the textbook) to illustrate the volume of drugs seized in Middle and South America.

Questions
  a. Explain why people are involved in the drug trade in Middle and South America. Discuss the small-scale growers, public figures, and cartels. Use the map you created to help discuss economic reasons for involvement in the drug trade.

b. Explain the effects of the drug trade in Middle and South America. Be sure to give examples of both positive and negative effects.

c. Based on the data presented about trends in cocaine seizures (Figure 3.15), choose one country whose seizures are increasing by 10 percent or more and speculate as to the future of the drug trade in this specific country.

d. Do some quick news article research on the Internet related to the recent rise in Mexico's drug trade and violence. Speculate on the impacts it will have on the region, and on the United States.

3. Economy and well-being of Middle and South America

GDP per capita masks the very wide disparity of wealth in the region. Some HDI rankings are higher partly because education is somewhat more available across gender and class. Female earnings compared to male earnings are low overall, but are higher in some countries because their governments support education and equal opportunity for women.

- Map GDP per capita on the blank map of Middle and South America by shading the countries according to the legend in Figure 3.18.
- Write L (for very low or low), M (for medium-low, medium, or medium-high), or H (for high or very high) for the HDI ranking for all countries in the region (Figure 3.18).
- Use a graduated symbol (e.g., from small to large squares) to map "female earned income as a % of male income" (Figure 3.18) using the following three categories: 12-39%; 40-57%; 58-84%.

Questions

a. Explain the general relationship you would *expect* for the three variables you mapped.

b. Do you see any discrepancies between GDP and HDI (e.g., high GDP with low ranking HDI or low GDP with high ranking HDI)? Explain why these discrepancies may exist *in general*.

c. One might assume that a country with high GDP per capita would also have a high ranking HDI and gender equality. Which three countries stand out the most (i.e., have the most discrepancies)? Explain the discrepancies for these specific countries based on history or current conditions.

d. After examining the "2004-2007 richest 10% to poorest 10%" ratio from Table 3.2, does it help to explain any of these anomalies?

SAMPLE EXAM QUESTIONS

The following are sample questions to help you review for an exam. Answers are found in the back of this study guide.

1. Which of the following is NOT a key difference between North America and Middle and South America?
a) Middle and South America are larger than North America.
b) Middle and South America have a more varied environment.
c) Middle and South America have a larger indigenous population.
d) Middle and South America have a less varied level of human well-being.

2. Which of the following features of the physical environment contributes least to the climate in Middle and South America?
a) ocean currents
b) topography
c) global wind patterns
d) soil type

3. All of the following are contributing to deforestation in Middle and South America except for:
a) the clearing of land to raise cattle and cash crops.
b) the logging of hardwoods.
c) the extraction of minerals and oil.
d) the increased volcanic activity in the region.

4. All of the following are goals of NAFTA except:
a) the creation of SAPs so that member nations can pay off their debts.
b) improving working conditions across the region.
c) establishing mutually advantageous trade rules.
d) creating expanded markets for the goods and services produced in North America.

5. Which of the following has NOT been a widespread response of small-scale farmers who were displaced by large cash-crop enterprises?
a) They migrated to cities.
b) They found work on plantations.
c) They formed partnerships that bought into the newer, larger farms.
d) They took over the unused areas of farms.

6. Which of the following types of government dominates the Middle and South America region?
a) communism
b) military dictatorship
c) democracy
d) populist dictatorship

7. Which of the following did not play a role in Middle and South America's population explosion in the twentieth century?
a) improved living conditions
b) cultural mores that encouraged reproduction
c) religious beliefs that discourage family planning
d) increased colonization and migration from abroad

8. All of the following are elements of machismo except:
a) polygamy.
b) household leadership.
c) attractiveness to women.
d) storytelling.

9. Why don't authorities in Middle and South America evict squatters after a settlement is established on private land?
a) They are concerned for the squatters' welfare.
b) They are a huge portion of the community and authorities are afraid of confrontation.
c) There is no legal basis for eviction.
d) The landowners don't mind having the squatters.

10. All of the following are contributing to deforestation in Middle and South America except for:
a) the clearing of land to raise cattle and cash crops.
b) the logging of hardwoods.
c) the extraction of minerals and oil.
d) the increased volcanic activity in the region.

MIDDLE & S. AMERICA

	Miles	
0		1000
0	Kilometers	1600

MIDDLE & S. AMERICA

0   Miles   1000
0 Kilometers 1600

MIDDLE & S. AMERICA

Miles
0   1000
Kilometers
0   1600

CHAPTER FOUR
Europe

LEARNING OBJECTIVES

After reading the chapter and working through this study guide, you should understand how the textbook's nine thematic concepts relate to Europe.

- Climate change: Understand why the climate in Europe is reasonably mild despite its northerly latitude and predict changes in lifestyles that evolve with both gradual and sudden changes in the climate.
- Democratization: Know how the supranational organization, the European Union (EU), promotes economic, political, and related social integration, all to eliminate regional disparities and provide a high standard of living in all democratic member- countries.
- Development: Understand the role that the European Union (EU) is playing to guarantee that its member countries provide equitable living and working opportunities for all citizens, including those of varying ethnic and cultural groups.
- Food: Be able to match various forms of agricultural practices with the different climatic regions of Europe. At the same time, understand why various climates have helped to influence regional cuisine.
- Gender: Know that while gender roles are gradually changing, women must still cope with challenges of day care, flexible working hours, gendered work roles, and domestic responsibilities when they work outside the home.
- Globalization: An understanding of Europe's role in exploration and colonization will help you to identify the underlying capital that brought about the industrial revolution which made Europe a global economic leader. Also understand Europe's current reliance on outside sources of material to maintain its high level of development.
- Population: The aging of the European population means ever-increasing reliance on guest workers (temporary migrants) who perform many of the region's menial jobs. Understand that these new immigrants often face difficulties with acculturation and assimilation into majority cultures, which themselves are seeking to maintain national identities in the face of the homogenization associated with EU membership.
- Urbanization: Understand the reasons why Europe has a high population density living primarily in urban settings with a very high standard of living, despite a diminishing resource base.
- Water: Know that environmentalists in Europe are focusing on sustaining livable environments and encouraging regional cooperation when dealing with pollution in the seas, rivers, and air.

KEY TERMS

The following terms are in **bold** in the textbook. Page numbers for each term can be found in the Chapter Key Terms list at the end of the textbook chapter. In the space next to the term (or on a separate sheet or flash cards), you can fill in the definitions for reference or quiz yourself for exam review. Definitions are found in the glossary of the textbook, as well as in the sidebars on the page they first appear.

assimilation

Biosphere

capitalism

central planning

cold war

Common Agricultural Program (CAP)

Communism

cool humid continental climate

cultural homogenization

double day

economies of scale

euro

European Union (EU)

exclave (Subregions textbook version only)

Green

guest workers

Holocaust

humanism

iron curtain

Mediterranean climate

mercantilism

nationalism

North Atlantic Drift

North Atlantic Treaty Organization (NATO)

Roma

Schengen Accord

social welfare (in the EU, social protection)

subsidies

temperate midlatitude climate

welfare state

REVIEW QUESTIONS

The following review questions are related directly to the textbook material. These questions can be used to help you prepare for an exam, or you may want to read through the questions before you begin reading the textbook, quizzing yourself after you complete each section.

The Geographic Setting

1. What is meant by the description of the region as "peninsulas upon peninsulas"? What is the climatic impact of such extensive contact with oceans and seas?
2. Of the three types of landforms in this region (mountains, uplands, and lowlands), which are most closely associated with current human activities? What are some of these activities and where is the human impact most profound?
3. What unique adaptations have humans made to the three main climate zones (temperate midlatitude, Mediterranean, and cool humid continental)?
4. If Europe's natural landscape has been so extensively transformed by humans over time, then what particular role can the Green movement play? What do you see in the Green movement that may serve as important role models for the rest of the world?

5. How does the reliance on Russian energy resources present diplomatic and economic challenges? What significant efforts are some European countries making to adapt various forms of renewable energy to meet their energy needs?

6. What explains the fact that pollution in all forms is highest in the former Communist states of central and north Europe? What indicators show important improvements in reduction of pollution in these former Communist states?

7. Describe the physical geography characteristics and the social, economic, and political issues that may explain the high rates of pollution in the Black, Baltic, and Mediterranean Seas.

8. Summarize the virtual water impact of the average European consumer. How does Europe's virtual water impact affect its total impact on the Biosphere?

9. How were the Industrial Revolution and the process of colonialism linked? How did the process of colonialism accelerate globalization?

10. Most European governments operate within a welfare state. What is the rationale for becoming a welfare state and what is a government's role in such a setting? What are the challenges this form of government must face?

Current Geographic Issues

11. What are the historical economic influences that gave rise to the European Union (EU) and support its continued expansion? Despite growth of the EU, what remains as the central reason for the establishment of the EU? How was the concept of economies of scale achieved through the formation of the EU?

12. From the perspective of individual countries, what are some negative or more challenging aspects of attaining and maintaining membership in the EU? Besides discussing the economic challenges, please address cultural challenges, too.

13. Why was the euro established as the common currency? Identify two countries that elected not to use the euro. What rationale did these countries provide for retaining their own currency? What are the disadvantages?

14. How does the Common Agricultural Program (CAP) protect and guarantee the Europeans a constant food supply? What influenced the growth of corporate agriculture in this region?

15. The growth of the service industry is associated with increased employment opportunities. What are some of these opportunities? What is the overall mixture of high-paying versus low-paying jobs?

16. Even though Europe has a very high population density, most people enjoy a high standard of living. What aspects of Europe's urbanization allow for a high quality of life amidst high population densities?

17. What burdens are placed on a society when the population of a country achieves a negative rate of natural increase? What are some coping mechanisms?

18. What trends do the textbook authors suggest are occurring because of more open borders and changing perspectives on citizenship requirements for immigrants?

19. What are some case studies that suggest some ethnic groups are coerced into assimilation? How is this coercion contradictory to the core values of the EU?

20. Describe the double day in the context of a twenty-first century European woman who has attained a graduate degree, is employed, is married, and has a child. Link the role of women as workers, caregivers, and providers in the context of the differing welfare systems in Europe.

CRITICAL THINKING EXERCISES

The following questions ask you to apply the ideas and principles you learned from the textbook to new situations.

1. Marginalized groups in European countries

After reading about the daily lives of so many Europeans as portrayed in the various case studies, identify one group of people that you think faces the most challenges in improving their status of human well-being. Your choice may be based on a theme such as ethnicity, gender, rurality, age, religion, or nationality. You may want to do some outside reading on the different subregions: West Europe, South Europe, North Europe, and Central Europe.

- Explain why you selected this particular group.
- Identify the issues or policies that are marginalizing this particular group. What is the kind of marginalization that this group is experiencing?
- Suggest at least three ways to improve the lives of this particular group.
- Suggest challenges that will be faced in bringing about the change.
- Identify the role that the EU might play in bringing this marginalized group into mainstream economic and political consideration without sacrificing its uniqueness.

2. Europe's negative rate of natural increase: How do you fit in?

Many European countries are experiencing a negative rate of natural increase. Soon a significant percent of the population will be aging.

- Select a European country that is currently experiencing a negative rate of population growth. Suppose that you are a citizen of that country. Use the *CIA World Factbook* at www.cia.gov/cia/publications/factbook for necessary data and information.
- Find the population pyramid for that country on the U.S. Census Bureau's Web site: www.census.gov/ipc/www/idb/. Once you log into this page then click on the "Data Access" in the center box which will take you to the data and population pyramid site for the world's countries. At this site you can select your country.
- Note the bar that would represent your gender and age group on that country's population pyramid, and compare it to the bars that represent the aging population.
- Suggest responsibilities that people your age might face as a consequence of a growing population of elderly in your selected country.
- Suggest possible impacts that people your age might face as a consequence of a growing population of elderly in your selected country.

3. Urban life in Europe

Europe is a highly urbanized region. Tourists from around the world are attracted by the art, music, and architecture of the great cities of this region. Assume that you have an opportunity to study abroad in a European city for one semester.

- Identify one city where you would like to study and specify the university that you would attend. Explain why you selected this university, its city, and its country.
- Using information from the textbook and visits to Web sites for the country, the city, and the university you have selected, explain how five examples of urban living there might be different from the lifestyle you now experience as a student.
- Explain how your examples match the textbook's discussion of urbanization in Europe.

4. Supranational transitions in Europe: Challenges of integration

With the ever-increasing role of the European Union in the daily lives of Europeans, one wonders how citizens of individual countries are responding to such regional changes as the euro, a common passport, open borders, and the influence of a homogeneous Euro-pop culture. Reflect on your own personal sense of nationalism and decide if you could support a United States of North America that included Canada, the United States, and Mexico.

- Identify the challenges you would face in developing loyalty to a supranational political structure.
- Suggest some expanded opportunities you might enjoy as a consequence of an expanded supranational political structure.

5. Impact of EU membership on a selected country

Select a country that joined the EU in the twenty-first century. The official EU Web site (www.europa.eu) will help you with this information. You may want to investigate your selected country's official Web site as well. Respond to the following questions:

- What are the positive and negative aspects of EU membership for the country you selected? Note some interesting case studies provided in the textbook.
- How has membership in the EU for the country you selected fostered greater linkages within the EU and the rest of the globe?
- What major problems is the country facing and how can its EU membership help it to solve those problems? Again, note some of the case studies provided in the textbook.

IMPORTANT PLACES

The following places are featured in the chapter. Make sure you can locate all of them on a map. Blank outline maps can be found on the textbook's Web site: www.whfreeman.com/pulsipher5e. Also, to prepare for quizzes and exams, write a few important facts about each place in the space provided.

Physical Features

1. Adriatic Sea

2. Alps

3. Arctic Ocean

4. Atlantic Ocean

5. Baltic Sea

6. Black Sea

7. Corsica

8. Danube River

9. Elbe River

10. English Channel

11. Iberian Peninsula

12. Mediterranean Basin

13. Mediterranean Sea

14. Morava River

15. North European Plain

16. North Sea

17. Rhine River

18. Strait of Gibraltar

Regions/Countries/States/Provinces

19.   Albania

20.   Almeria

21.   Andorra

22.   Austria

23.   Balkans

24.   Belgium

25.   Bosnia-Herzegovina

26.   Bulgaria

27.   Catalonia

28.   Central Europe

29.   Croatia

30.   Cyprus

31.   Czech Republic

32.   Denmark

33.   England

34.   Estonia

35.   Europe

36.   Finland

37.   France

38.   Germany

39.   Greece

40. Hungary

41. Iceland

42. Ireland (Republic of)

43. Italy

44. Kosovo

45. Latvia

46. Lithuania

47. Luxembourg

48. Macedonia

49. Malta

50. Montenegro

51. Netherlands

52. Northern Ireland

53. North Europe

54. Norway

55. Poland

56. Portugal

57. Romania

58. Schleswig-Holstein

59. Scotland

60. Serbia

61. Slovakia

62. Slovenia

63. South Europe

64. Spain

65. Sweden

66. Switzerland

67. United Kingdom

68. Upper Silesia

69. Vatican City

70. Wales

71. West Europe

Cities/Urban Areas
72. Amsterdam

73. Antwerp

74. Athens

75. Barcelona

76. Belfast

77. Belgrade

78. Benidorm

79. Berlin

80. Bern

81. Bratislava

82. Brussels

83.   Bucharest

84.   Budapest

85.   Campo de Dalia

86.   Copenhagen

87.   Cordoba

88.   Dijon

89.   Dublin

90.   Frankfurt

91.   Hamburg

92.   Heldsburg

93.   Helsinki

94.   Koper

95.   Krakow

96.   Kuhtai

97.   Le Havre

98.   Lisbon

99.   Ljubljana

100.   London

101.   Luxembourg (city)

102.   Madrid

103.   Marseille

104.   Nicosia

105.   Oslo

106.   Paris

107.   Plymouth

108.   Podgorica

109.   Poznan

110.   Prague

111.   Reykjavik

112.   Riga

113.   Rome

114.   Rotterdam

115.   Saarschleife

116.   Sarajevo

117.   Skopje

118.   Sofia

119.   Southampton

120.   Stockholm

121.   Tallinn

122.   Turin

123.   Tirane

124.   Valletta

125.   Viareggio

126.   Vienna

127. Vilnius

128. Warsaw

129. Zagreb

MAPPING EXERCISES

The following mapping exercises are designed to improve your knowledge of the location of places, underscore why they are important, and clarify how they relate to one another. Some questions will ask you to locate places, compare maps, or fill in data; others will test your understanding of *why* you were asked to map the features that you did. Use the blank outline maps at the end of the chapter to complete these exercises. Additional blank outline maps can be found on the textbook's Web site: www.whfreeman.com/pulsipher5e.

1. River basins, population, and pollution

Rivers play an important role in the continued success of European economies. Significant rivers flow through several countries and provide valuable transportation access. Manufacturing districts grew up in areas that formerly provided important industrial materials. Unfortunately, these valuable rivers are also highly polluted. Using the map of Europe, complete the following:

- Label the following rivers: the Danube, the Elbe, the Rhine, the Seine, and the Thames.
- Using the map of population density (Photo Essay 4.5), shade the areas (in red) that have a population density greater than 250 persons per square kilometer (greater than 650 persons per square mile).
- Locate and label all cities with 3 million people or more (Photo Essay 4.6).
- Using Figure 4.4, shade the seas and water bodies that are exceptionally polluted.

Questions

    a. Using this mapped information, briefly describe the pattern and distribution of population.

    b. Is population concentrated in any particular location (for example, along the coasts, along major rivers, or in the interior)?

    c. Summarize the relationship among the five rivers, population concentrations, and highly polluted seas or oceans. What role do the rivers play in pollution of the larger water bodies?

    d. Suggest some changes that will still allow the rivers to be used as major arteries for transport while at the same time permitting successful cleanup and good stewardship along their channels and their deltas.

    e. Investigate the role of the EU in helping to reverse the consequences of water pollution.

2. Immigration, Aging, and Economic Success: Is there a relationship?

Do countries with high levels of aging attract immigrants who can do the work that the aging no longer can perform? Do countries with high GDP per capita attract immigrants who have expectations of high-paying jobs?

- On an outline map of Europe, and using appropriate shades of gray, map the 2005 immigration data for each country as shown in Figure 4.16.
- On the same map, and using graduated circles, map the GDP per capita of the countries in Europe using information from Figure 4.12.
- Finally refer to the CIA Factbook Field Listing: Age Structure at www.cia.gov/library/publications/the-world-factbook/fields/2010.html to identify the percent of each European country's population over age 65 and use cross-hatches of appropriate widths to indicate the percent of each country's population that is over 65.

Questions

    a. Study the map you have created that shows three different sets of information. What is the relationship between immigration and aging and between immigration and GDP per capita. Does the map help you to draw any conclusions? Explain your response.

3. Women's empowerment in Europe

Some European countries have shown exemplary progress in bringing women into equally responsible positions in government and related socioeconomic strata of society. However, these countries may not be representative of the entire European region.

- Carefully observe Figure 4.22 C (Female Earned Income as Percent of Male Earned Income).
- Carefully observe the map in Figure 4.21 that represents each of the five welfare/protection systems found in Europe.

Questions

    a. Describe any patterns that suggest a correspondence between certain welfare regimes and women's overall income equity in different European countries.

    b. Based on your reading of the textbook, what do you think is the driving force in areas where women are highly empowered and actively engaged in political agendas?

    c. After reading the textbook sections on gender and social welfare/protection systems, suggest a country in Europe that could serve as a good role model for promoting women's empowerment. Give three reasons why you selected this country.

SAMPLE EXAM QUESTIONS

The following are sample questions to help you review for an exam. Answers are found in the back of this study guide.

1. The entire European region is one giant _____ extending off the Eurasian continent.
a) archipelago
b) peninsula
c) atoll
d) island

2. Europe's moderate climate is largely due to:
a) the presence of numerous mountain ranges in its landmass.
b) the climate-moderating effects of the large bodies of water that surround it.
c) the Gulf Stream and the Jet Stream.
d) the atmospheric cooling effects of volcanic eruptions in Scandinavia.

3. In addition to industrial sites, cities, and transport spaces, what is the dominant land cover throughout Europe?
a) taiga forests and steppe lands
b) glacial rock and sandy soils
c) crops and pasture grass
d) tundra and subtropical forests

4. Which is not a major supplier of crude oil and natural gas to Europe?
a) Norway
b) Russia
c) the United States (Texas and Alaska)
d) the Middle East

5. Air pollution is heavy over the North European Plain due to all of the following factors except:
a) large population.
b) dense transport routes.
c) heavy industry.
d) radioactive particles created by nuclear energy.

6. Why are the Mediterranean and Black Seas prone to heavier loads of pollution than the Atlantic Ocean and North Sea?
a) The countries bordering the Black and Mediterranean Seas are home to industries that create higher levels of pollution.
b) Higher temperatures in the Atlantic Ocean and North Sea cause pollution to biodegrade much more quickly.
c) The Atlantic Ocean and North Sea are part of or closely connected to the circulating flow of the world ocean, allowing them to disperse pollution more easily.
d) The Mediterranean and Black Seas support heavier populations, which create more human and industrial waste.

7. What is true of Paris and London?
a) They are, although well-known, relatively small with populations under 1 million each.
b) They are unimportant on the global scale.
c) They are world cities of cultural and economic significance.
d) They have been of global importance since Roman times.

8. The creation of the EU formalizes which of the following processes?
a) economic integration of Europe
b) rising self-sufficiency of European countries
c) spread of European influence into northern Africa
d) the replacement of NATO by a similar European-led alliance

9. Which of the following is among the core ideas of the EU?
a) strengthen boundaries to increase productivity rates independently within member-countries
b) achieve economic and social integration
c) increase tariffs on European goods to generate funds for the welfare system
d) build power among European states to combat Communism

10. Which of the following is a likely result of a stable population with a low birth rate?
a) The economy expands over time.
b) Demand for high-skilled workers may go unmet.
c) Immigration to that nation decreases.
d) More people are available to care for the elderly.

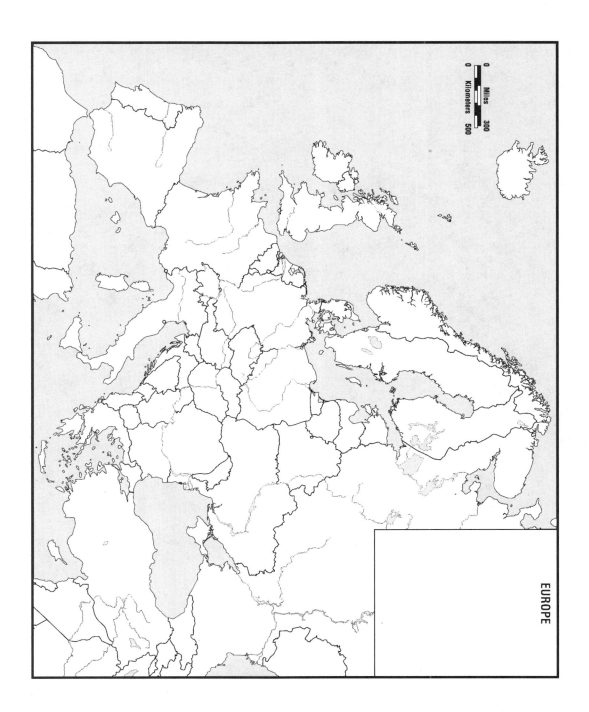

EUROPE

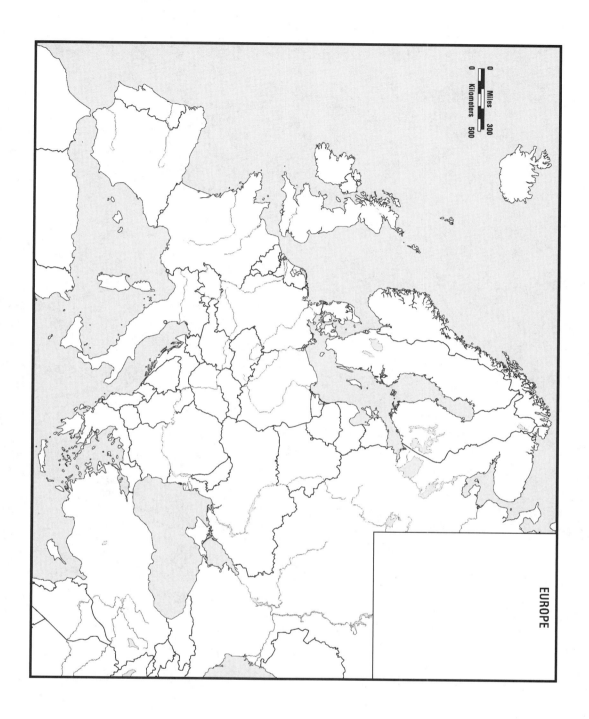

EUROPE

Europe

CHAPTER FIVE
Russia and the Post-Soviet States

LEARNING OBJECTIVES

After reading the chapter and working through this study guide, you should understand how the textbook's nine thematic concepts relate to Russia and the post-Soviet states.

- Climate change: Understand how the exploitation and development of resources has damaged the region's environment and affected climate change. Understand how the extent of this damage affects quality of life, not just in this region but globally. Note in particular how the Central Asian states will be affected by global warming.
- Democratization: Understand the challenges of developing democratic systems of governance. Be able to explain the role of civic responsibility in maintaining democratic systems.
- Development: Understand why economic transition to market economies based on capitalism continues to be a difficult challenge. Be able to identify impacts on the environment as economies seek to develop resources.
- Food: Understand the challenges that this region faces in feeding masses of people. Identify the resources that can support high crop yield in this region. Understand the relationship between economic insecurity and nutrition levels.
- Gender: Be able to identify the special difficulties for women as a consequence of the transition to market economies. Understand how prostitution affects women, and identify efforts to control this practice.
- Globalization: Understand how Russia and some of the post-Soviet states are linked to global partners through export of natural resources. Identify the economic impacts of high reliance on natural resource incomes.
- Population: Understand the reasons for profound demographic change in this region. Be able to identify the reasons for variations in birth rates and life expectancies among the post-Soviet states.
- Urbanization: Explain why primate cities continue to attract internal migrants while smaller cities are losing population. Understand the way in which cities are affected by highly polluting industrial activities.
- Water: Be able to explain the reliance on water in various subregions and the overall pollution of water bodies, including major rivers whose poisoned effluent is deposited into oceans and seas.

KEY TERMS

The following terms are in **bold** in the textbook. Page numbers for each term can be found in the Chapter Key Terms list at the end of the textbook chapter. In the space next to the term (or on a separate sheet or flash cards), you can fill in the definitions for reference or quiz yourself for exam review. Definitions are found in the glossary of the textbook, as well as in the sidebars on the page they first appear.

Bolsheviks

capitalists

Caucasia

centrally planned or socialist economy

Communism

Communist Party

czar

Gazprom

glasnost

Group of Eight (G8)

Mongols

nomadic pastoralists

nonpoint sources of pollution

oligarchs

perestroika

permafrost

privatization

proletariat

Russian Federation

Russification

Slavs

Soviet Union

steppes

taiga

tundra

underemployment

Union of Soviet Socialist Republics (USSR)

REVIEW QUESTIONS

The following review questions are related directly to the textbook material. These questions can be used to help you prepare for an exam, or you may want to read through the questions before you begin reading the textbook, quizzing yourself after you complete each section.

The Geographic Setting

1. Moving from the western border of this region to its eastern border, identify the bands of landforms. As you list each landform, identify its particular agriculture, natural resource base, and any special adaptations the citizens of the region have made in order to survive.
2. Discuss the climatic conditions that make European Russia and Caucasia the agricultural backbone of the region.
3. Russia is called the epitome of a continental climate. What are two characteristics of that continentality? List three impacts on human activity in such a climate.
4. How is the region's environmental plight rooted in Communist drives to industrialize the USSR?
5. What did the Russian environmentalist mean when he said, "When people became more involved with their stomachs, they forgot about ecology"?
6. Name two ways the river systems of this region help promote development and two ways that they are seen to hinder development.
7. The Russian-Mongol interaction was historically one of domination and exchange. How did both sides benefit from mutual cooperation?

8. Name two conditions in Russia that helped to promote the rise of Communism. Name two conditions that ultimately led to the downfall of Communism in this region.

9. What were the misguided practices of the Communist command economy that ultimately led to its failure? How was the command economy an explanation for the lack of management and technical innovation during the Soviet era?

Current Geographic Issues

10. Who are the oligarchs and how did they rise to power? In what spheres do they continue to exercise the most influence?

11. What roles have natural gas and oil reserves begun to play in the economies of this region? Identify at least two pros and two cons of such a reliance on these natural resources.

12. Describe the major transition in agricultural production following the end of the Soviet Union. Note the gains and losses that agricultural production has experienced in the last twenty years. What role does the individual family garden play in relation to nutrition?

13. How is economic change since the dissolution of the USSR reflected in household well-being? What are short-term and long-term challenges faced by households?

14. While entrepreneurism is a valid economic activity in a capitalist economy, what are the roadblocks to successful small business development in this region? How do informal sector activities relate to entrepreneurism and how do they relate to the black market of Soviet days?

15. What role do the *securocrats* or *siloviki* play in the Russian governmental bureaucracy? What other governmental activities that you read about in the textbook suggest that democratization must face many challenges before it is fully characteristic of the states in this region? Justify your choices.

16. This region claims to be part of the developed world, yet some of the population patterns discussed contradict this assertion. What are three of these contradictory facts and what circumstances gave rise to them?

17. What are some of the reasons why male life spans in the Russian Federation are now the shortest of those in the world's industrialized countries?

18. In what ways are the aging members of these states particularly affected by economic reforms?

19. How are the universal stereotypical roles of women reinforced in the current economic situation in Russia? How is this detrimental to women's roles in society and at home?

20. How does the loss of jobs in government-owned industries also represent the loss of a critical social safety net?

CRITICAL THINKING EXERCISES

The following questions ask you to apply the ideas and principles you learned from the textbook to new situations.

1. Life in Russia for a university student

After reading the sections in the textbook that discuss the well-being and opportunities for the Russian population, you may have thought about how you would or would not cope with comparable circumstances. The textbook makes several references to youth and young adults.

- Place yourself in Russia and consider the quality of life you might have, as well as your prospects for the future, if you were a student or working adult there.
- Where would you live and what kinds of work or internships would you most likely find upon completing your education?
- Identify the impacts of massive pollution on you as a college student. Identify the impacts of current economic reforms on you based on your gender and age. What would be your future prospects for economic security and good health in this society?

2. Growing old in societies under transition

During the Soviet era, adequate retirements were guaranteed, and workers had expectations of reasonable pensions during their retirement years. With the transition to market economies and the decline of state-owned corporations, the elderly in these countries are struggling to survive.

- Investigate how the elderly who worked in former state-owned companies are managing to survive in one of the countries of this region.
- Identify the efforts on the part of central governments to provide for these marginalized members of society.
- Identify how the current workers in privatized companies are planning for their own retirements, and compare the new system to the old.
- You may want to read the country snapshot by referring to the CIA World Factbook www.cia.gov/cia/publications/factbook section for a country of your choice.

3. Humans can change climate!

The desertification that is occurring around the Aral Sea is a classic case study of human-induced deserts (also called anthropological desertification).

- What are the policies and actions at the national and subregional levels that have brought on this climate change?
- What factors of daily life have experienced substantial change as a consequence of climatic change in the region surrounding the Aral Sea?
- What are some steps that could be followed to reverse the process while providing sustainable options for economic livelihoods?
- Who should take responsibility for rectifying this situation? Suggest some roles that citizens can have in this process.

4. Individual efforts to enhance nutrition

The textbook includes an informative note on urban gardening in this region. Even during the Soviet era, citizens were allowed to have gardens in small plots, even to sell some of the produce in local open-air markets.

- Investigate the history of the *dacha* in Russia. Then investigate community garden projects in the United States. You might even search out a local community garden near your campus.
- What do you see as similar, especially the reasons for participation in urban gardening?
- What are some differences between the urban gardens of Russia and the community gardens in U.S. cities? Why do these differences exist?
- What would be a factor to motivate you to participate in a community garden and would that be similar to those motivating people in Russia who practice urban gardening? What would be some differences?

5. Natural resources in Russia and the newly independent states

Oil and natural gas reserves are abundant in this region. Russia has used the revenues from natural gas and oil sales to help ease its international debt crisis. Some of the newly independent states that have oil or natural gas reserves are seeking trading partners in the global community.

- What role do these resources play in Russia's interaction with Europe and the United States? What other industrializing countries are courting this region in order to be trading partners for the energy resources? How can Russia use the global need for energy resources to its advantage? How do these choices harm or help its international standing?
- In the long term, what alternate paths should these resource-rich countries take in order to be economically viable when their oil and gas reserves are depleted?

IMPORTANT PLACES

The following places are featured in the chapter. Make sure you can locate all of them on a map. Blank outline maps can be found on the textbook's Web site: www.whfreeman.com/pulsipher5e. Also, to prepare for quizzes and exams, write a few important facts about each place in the space provided.

Physical Features

1. Altai Mountains

2. Amu Darya River

3. Aral Sea

4. Arctic Ocean

5. Baltic Sea

6. Black Sea

7. Carpathian Mountains

8. Caspian Sea

9. Caucasus Mountains

10. Central Siberian Plateau

11. Dneiper River

12. Eurasian Plate

13. Ferghana Valley

14. Hindu Kush Mountains

15. Kamchatka Peninsula

16. Lake Baikal

17. North European Plain

18. Lena River

19. Ob River

20. Pacific Mountain Zone

21. Pacific Ocean

22. Pamir Mountains

23. Sakalin Island

24. Sea of Okhotsk

25. Siberia

26. Sikhote Alin

27. Syr Darya River

28. Tien Shan Mountains

29. Ural Mountains

30. Volga River

31. West Siberian Plain

32. White Sea

33. Yenisey River

Regions/Countries/States/Provinces
34. Abkhazia

35. Armenia

36. Azerbaijan

37. Belarus

38. Buryatya

39. Caucasia (Caucasian Republics/States)

40. Central Asia (Central Asian Republics/States)

41. Chechnya

42. European Russia

43. Georgia

44. Kaliningrad

45. Kazakhstan

46. Kyrgyzstan

47. Moldova

48. Russia

49. Russian Far East

50. South Ossetia

51. Tajikistan

52. Tatarstan

53. Turkmenistan

54. Ukraine

55. Uzbekistan

Cities/Urban Areas
56. Almaty

57. Angarsk

58. Ashkhabad

59. Astana

60. Baku

61. Bishkek

62. Chelyabinsk

63. Chernobyl

64. Chisinau

65. Donetsk

66. Dushanbe

67. Dzerzhinsk

68. Groznyy

69. Irkutsk

70. Kharkiv

71. Kiev

72. Krasnoyarsk

73. Minsk

74. Moscow

75. Norilsk

76. Novosibirsk

77. Pripyat

78. St. Petersburg

79. Tashkent

80. Tbilisi

81. Yekaterinburg

82. Yerevan

MAPPING EXERCISES

The following mapping exercises are designed to improve your knowledge of the location of places, underscore why they are important, and clarify how they relate to one another. Some questions will ask you to locate places, compare maps, or fill in data; others will test your understanding of *why* you were asked to map the features that you did. Use the blank outline maps at the end of the chapter to complete these exercises. Additional blank outline maps can be found on the textbook's Web site: www.whfreeman.com/pulsipher5e.

1. Industry, pollution, and populations at risk
Industrial pollution reduces the quality of life for citizens living and working near industrial complexes. We can more carefully identify populations who are at risk of the impacts of industrial pollution by using maps to generate information.

- Construct a map that shows areas with population densities of 261 people or more per square mile (101 people or more per square kilometer) (Photo Essay 5.5). A good symbolization would be shading using the darkest shade to represent highest population concentrations.
- Overlay areas of high industrial development (Figure 5.13). Categorize these by type of industrial region as designated in the legend for Figure 5.13.

- Overlay areas of oil and natural gas-producing regions (Figure 5.14). Again use a unique symbol, such as cross-hatching.
- Finally, overlay areas of human impacts (Photo Essay 5.2) using unique symbols for high impact and medium-high impact.

Questions
    a. What appears to be a major source of employment for people in the densely populated areas?
    b. What conclusions can you draw about environmental impacts on health? What are the governmental responsibilities for citizens' health?
    c. Identify three ways this region can cope with the environmental impacts of industrialization, resource extraction, and production?

2. Population issues in Russia and the post-Soviet states

By mapping demographic data by country, you should be able to arrive at some conclusions about population growth in this region.

- Using the CIA World Factbook at www.cia.gov/cia/publications/factbook, construct a map that portrays the birth rate for each country in this region. Use graduated circles to represent birth rates.
- Refer to Figure 5.24A (Map of human well-being) to shade GDP per capita for each country. Be sure the lightest shade represents the lowest value and the darkest shade represents the highest value.
- Refer to Figure 5.24B (Map of human well-being) and use diagonal lines (///) to indicate the seven HDI rankings. Use closely spaced lines to represent those countries with good HDI rankings and use widely spaced lines to represent those countries with poor HDI rankings.

Questions
    a. Use this mapped information to help explain why some countries have a decreasing birth rate and why others have an increasing birth rate.
    b. If GDP and HDI are not fully explanatory for some of the countries, suggest three other factors that might explain those countries' birth rates.

3. Water and oil: Critical resources that affect international relations in the Central Asian Republics

Control and access to headwaters or upstream waters of the major rivers of the Central Asian Republics may be a deciding factor in the continuation of cotton production in the region. Oil pipeline routes may change as newly independent countries develop international ties with countries that were never part of the former USSR.

- Label the Central Asian Republics and label their neighbors.
- Use the regional map (Figure 5.1) to label and outline the rivers (in blue) that supply water to Central Asia's irrigation projects. Shade in all the countries that are drained by these rivers.
- On Figure 5.16 (map of agriculture), observe the cash crops in the Central Asia valleys. These are most likely cash crops, cotton primarily. Shade these areas.

- Use the oil and natural gas resource map (Figure 5.14) to cross-hatch the location of oil- and gas-producing areas in this region.
- Also from Figure 5.14, draw in red the current oil and gas pipelines that move these resources to shipping ports. Using a second color, suggest alternative routes that lie outside of the region for moving this oil to shipping ports.

Questions

a. Identify countries in this region that will have to develop some basis for negotiating use of the water from these rivers. How will upstream countries have an advantage? What counterarguments or possible offers can the downstream countries (where the rivers drain last) provide in order to assure access to the water?

b. Make an argument for how the new pipelines you suggested would be the most plausible considering international relations in the region, international demand, security, and certainly environmental sensitivity. The map in Figure 5.4 may help you with your decisions about international relations between Central Asia countries and their neighbors.

SAMPLE EXAM QUESTIONS

The following are sample questions to help you review for an exam. Answers are found in the back of this study guide.

1. Which one of the following features on the Eurasian physical landscape separates European Russia and Western Siberia?
a) Volga River
b) Ural Mountains
c) Aral Sea
d) Ob River

2. Which one of the following describes Russia's continental climate?
a) Cool summers and warm winters
b) Hot summers and cold winters
c) Hot summers and warm winters
d) Cold summers and cold winters

3. What type is the dominant groundcover in Russia's steppe lands?
a) Coniferous forest
b) Desert scrub
c) Grasses
d) Temperate rain forest

4. Which of the following is NOT one of the main efforts of Europe and the United States aimed at bringing Russia into closer formal association with established trading institutions?
a) Inviting Russia to join the World Trade Organization
b) Inviting Russia to increase its participation in the meetings of the Group of Eight
c) Encouraging Russia to work toward conformity with European standards by admitting former Russian allies to the European Union (EU)
d) Inviting Russia to join the EU

5. Which of the following describes the primary spatial growth of the Russian Empire beginning in the 1500s?
a) From Mongolia to the north and west
b) From Kazan to the north and west
c) From Moscow to the south and east
d) From Petersburg to the south and west

6. In the Soviet Union, what institution provided most of one's basic social services?
a) Nongovernmental organizations
b) Work place
c) Extended family
d) Military

7. Which of the following is cited in the textbook as a major reason for falling birth rates during the 1990s in Russia?
a) The Russian government implemented population control policies.
b) Couples decided against having children because of bleak economic prospects.
c) There has been a significant increase in migration to cities where children are more of an economic liability.
d) High levels of environmental pollution have caused sterility in many women.

8. The environmental and climatic changes wrought by the diversion of water from the Syr Darya and Amu Darya rivers are reflected in which of the following phenomena?
a) Saltwater intrusion in the Black Sea
b) Shrinkage of the Aral Sea
c) Heavier and more frequent rains in Central Asia
d) Cooler average temperatures throughout Central Asia

9. In the Soviet Union, what type of economy governed the production, distribution, and consumption of goods?
a) Market
b) Feudal
c) Mercantile
d) Command

10. In which of the following subregions do most of Russia's citizens reside?
a) European Russia
b) Western Siberia
c) Central Siberia
d) Far East

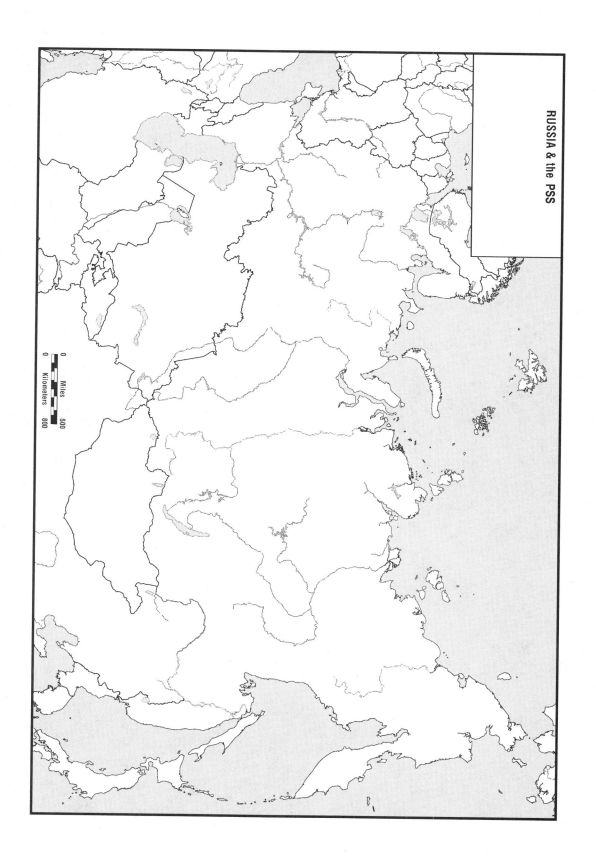

Miles

Kilometers

0

0

500

800

Russia and the Post-Soviet States

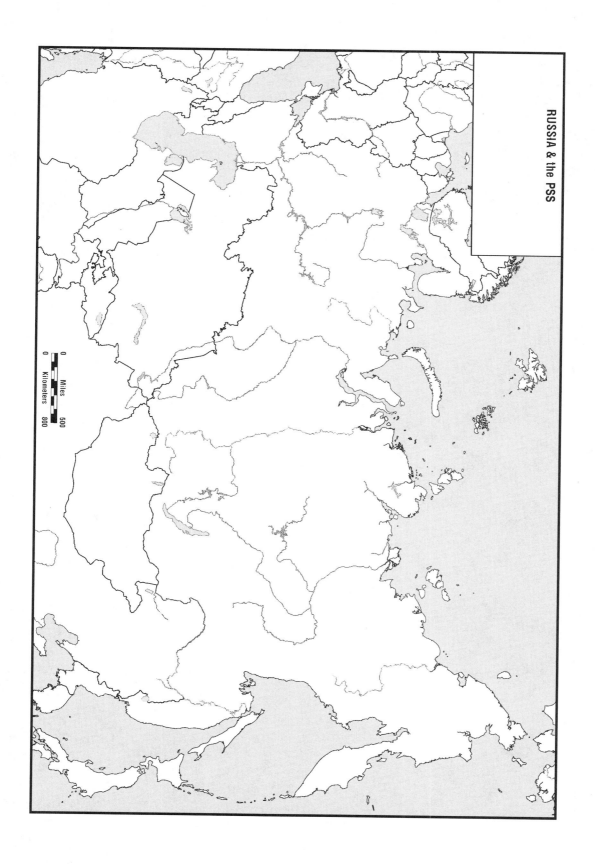

RUSSIA & the PSS

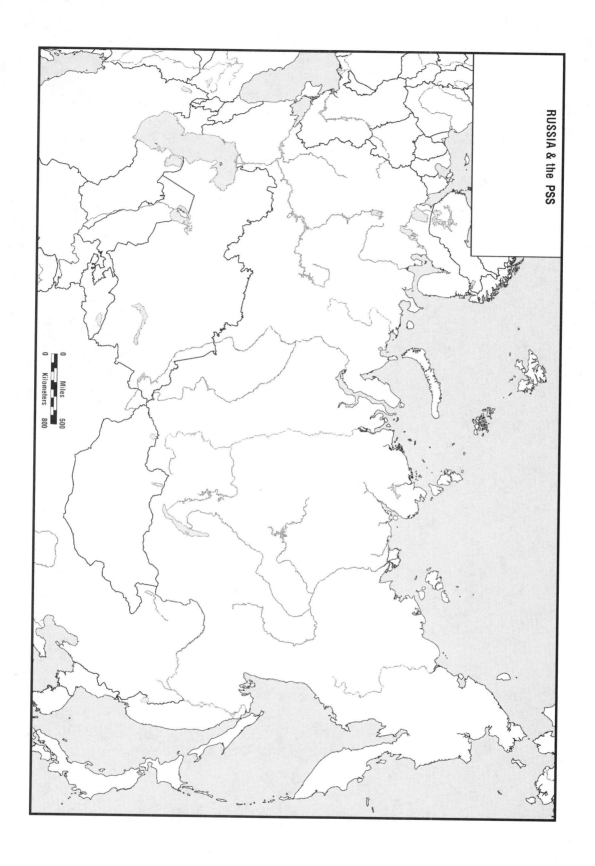

Russia and the Post-Soviet States

CHAPTER SIX
North Africa and Southwest Asia

LEARNING OBJECTIVES

After reading the chapter and working through this study guide, you should understand how the textbook's nine thematic concepts relate to North Africa and Southwest Asia.

- Climate change: Be able to speculate on how the growing population and vulnerability to climate change will affect water resources, flooding, and desertification.
- Democratization: Know how Islamic culture and beliefs affect government, law, and everyday behavior. Understand the causes and effects of the rise in Islamism, and its effects on democracy.
- Development: Know that oil revenue often results in significant income disparity. Know how countries' dependency on oil affects human well-being. Understand the challenges faced by countries in the region as they attempt to diversify their economies.
- Food: Understand how virtual water and imported food are changing the habitability of this region.
- Gender: Know some of the causes and effects of the restrictions on and seclusion of women. Understand why the patterns and degrees of seclusion vary greatly across the region. Be able to appreciate how the changing role of women will affect culture, politics, and economics in this region.
- Globalization: Know how OPEC helps to reduce the exploitation of fossil fuels in the region. Understand how economic diversification is related to globalization.
- Population: Know where and why populations are located where they are. Also understand how population growth is related to gender status.
- Urbanization: Understand how rural to urban, as well as international, migration is affecting cities in the region. Know how new forms of urbanization (e.g., Palm Jumeirah in Dubai) are affected by globalization, and how they are affecting the environment.
- Water: Know how residents and governments are attempting to make this largely desert region inhabitable for a growing population. Understand the effects these attempts are having on people, the economy, and the environment.

KEY TERMS

The following terms are in **bold** in the textbook. Page numbers for each term can be found in the Chapter Key Terms list at the end of the textbook chapter. In the space next to the term (or on a separate sheet or flash cards), you can fill in the definitions for reference or quiz yourself for exam review. Definitions are found in the glossary of the textbook, as well as in the sidebars on the page they first appear.

cartel

Christianity

desertification

diaspora

economic diversification

failed state (Subregions textbook version only)

female seclusion

Fertile Crescent

fossil fuel

Gulf States

hajj

intifada

Islam

Islamism

Judaism

monotheistic

Muslims

Occupied Palestinian Territories (OPT)

OPEC (Organization of Petroleum Exporting Countries)

patriarchal

polygyny

Qur'an (or Koran)

salinization

seawater desalinization

secular states

shari'a

sheikhs (Subregions textbook version only)

Shi'ite (or Shi'a)

sovereign-wealth funds

Sunni

the veil

theocratic states

West Bank barrier

Zionists

REVIEW QUESTIONS

The following review questions are related directly to the textbook material. These questions can be used to help you prepare for an exam, or you may want to read through the questions before you begin reading the textbook, quizzing yourself after you complete each section.

The Geographic Setting

1. Describe the climate-related function of the Atlas Mountains. How are the Atlas Mountains and the Sahara related? How do climate and human existence differ from one side of the mountains to the other?
2. How do Islamic beliefs affect the environment in this region? Why are environmental issues likely to increase in importance?
3. Discuss the concept of "virtual water" and its effects on the region's people and land.
4. The region's aridity has caused a number of environmental problems. How have humans historically coped with water scarcity? How is this changing? Why are water

problems getting worse, and how are countries dealing with these problems?

5. Desertification is an ecological disaster caused partly by human activity. What are some of the causes and effects of desertification?

6. Although Makkah (Mecca) is maintained as the holy city of Islam, in keeping with the tradition of hajj, Islam has spread through much of the world. How did this diffusion occur? What were some of the routes and means of diffusion? What are some of Islam's contributions?

7. How have colonization, Western domination, and oil wealth affected this region's economy, politics, and environment?

Current Geographic Issues

8. Although shari'a has many different interpretations, the Five Pillars of Islamic Practice are standard. Briefly explain each of them.

9. In many places in this region, how women occupy public and private spaces is strictly regulated. What are some of these restrictions, and how do these standards vary across the region and by social class? What is the logic behind these restrictions, and how are they enforced?

10. The size, aridity, and population density of this region greatly affect human settlement. Where do people live and why? What problems might an expanding population cause in cities?

11. As labor-intensive agriculture declines, the need for children also declines. Why do fertility rates remain high in this region? What would it take to lower them?

12. Trace the origins of urbanization in the region from ancient (e.g., Istanbul, Baghdad, Cairo, and Casablanca) to modern (e.g., Dubai). Where are immigrants coming from to present-day cities, and why?

13. Why is GDP per capita a poor measure of quality of life in this region? How is it possible for a country to have a low GDP but a high ranking HDI or high F/EIM? Give an example of a country in this situation. How is it possible for a country to have a high GDP but a low HDI or F/EIM? Give an example. What are several reasons why Israel is an exception to much of the inequality in this region?

14. What are some of the many economic and political barriers to peace and prosperity in this region?

15. The global economy is affected by more than just the buying and selling of goods and services. This region is heavily involved in the global economy, as workers are leaving some areas and migrating into others. Who is coming and who is leaving? What are the reasons for the emigration and immigration? What are the effects on the region's economy as well as on the global economy?

16. What was the purpose of establishing OPEC? Has it been a success? What are the positive and negative effects of it? What are its limitations and how could OPEC be more responsive to the social needs of the countries it represents? What will happen to OPEC countries as oil supplies decline worldwide?

17. Economic diversification can bring prosperity and stability. What are some of the reasons this region has had trouble developing economically?

18. Who are the Islamists? Why are revolutionary movements, including Islamic fundamentalism, on the rise? What does Islamism promise that secular governments do not?
19. How is democracy related to the press and media in this region? How is democracy related to gender in this region, and how is it changing?
20. What are the origins of the state of Israel? What are the many layered reasons for the conflict between Israelis and Palestinians today? How is the West Bank barrier both helping and hindering a resolution to this conflict?

CRITICAL THINKING EXERCISES

The following questions ask you to apply the ideas and principles you learned from the textbook to new situations.

1. Adaptations to the physical environment

The daily climate of this region can be harsh and dry; however, humans have learned to adapt and survive. Because water has always been in short supply in this arid region, cultural attitudes toward water differ greatly from those in North America.

- Temperatures in the Sahara can vary from below freezing to well over 100°. Heating and air-conditioning systems are not widely available in North Africa and Southwest Asia. What adaptations do people in North Africa and Southwest Asia make to survive in such harsh conditions?
- In Rub'al Khali, strong winds create dunes more than 2000 feet high. How do people protect themselves from these persistent winds and blowing sand?
- Only three major rivers flow in this region, and rainfall is infrequent and light from November to April. How do farmers and the nonfarming population deal with this water scarcity?
- Reflecting on the answers you have given, how would *you* cope with these harsh conditions if you did not have all the resources available to you (e.g., central heat and air, four solid walls around your house, and running water in it)?
- Finally, take a guess at how many gallons of water you use in a day. Remember brushing teeth, flushing toilets, showering, washing dishes, and just drinking a glass of water. After you have made an estimate, find out how much water you really use on a typical day by going to the Web site: http://ga.water.usgs.gov/edu/sq3.html. Did the amount you use surprise you?

2. Religion in daily life

The Five Pillars of Muslim Practice focus on how to live daily life.

- Consider the Five Pillars of Muslim Practice. If you follow a belief system other than Islam, do you have similar elements in your belief system? List the five most important "pillars" of your religion or belief system. Compare them to the Five Pillars of Muslim Practice.
- Do you find that your five "pillars" guide you through daily life, or do you practice

your belief system only during certain times or in certain spaces?

3. Restrictions on women in *your* daily life

In this region, some women are active in public life and government, while others lead secluded domestic lives with little opportunity for education.

- Men and boys usually interact in public spaces, while women usually inhabit secluded domestic spaces. In many countries in this region, women have to be accompanied by a male relative in public. How would this affect your daily life? How would this affect the education and career path you have chosen?
- Give some examples of material culture designed to seclude women from the public gaze in North Africa and Southwest Asia. Do you see any similar examples in your society? How would this seclusion affect your daily life and interactions?

4. Islamism in a globalizing world

Many Muslims see modern, Westernized culture as undermining important values. In reaction, religious fundamentalism is on the rise in many parts of the world.

- List some positive and negative impacts of each of the following perceived consequences of modernization: liberalization of women's roles, family instability, consumerism, and widening gaps between the rich and poor.
- Do you think Islamism and a reaffirmation of traditional values will reduce the negative impacts of modernization? Do you think Islamism can offer solutions to the region's problems and that things will be better if people return to strict interpretations of religious-based morality? Justify your response.
- How can modernization be combined with Muslim beliefs and values?
- What should be done about the rights of non-Muslims living in these societies?

5. Migration and refugees

Many immigrants in the region flee persecution, and then return after they are liberated. For example, 700,000 Jews were allowed to leave the former Soviet Union and enter Israel in the 1990s. However, because of the creation of the state of Israel in 1948, as many as 2 million Palestinians were displaced from their homeland.

- Why do you think Israel is such an important place for Jews?
- Where did the Palestinians go after leaving what is now Israel? What might their lives have been like because of this forced migration? What might life have been like for those Palestinians who stayed?
- What are the long-term effects of this migration on the Palestinians and on Israel?
- What would this forced migration be like for you to experience?

IMPORTANT PLACES

The following places are featured in the chapter. Make sure you can locate all of them on a map. Blank outline maps can be found on the textbook's Web site: www.whfreeman.com/pulsipher5e. Also, to prepare for quizzes and exams, write a few important facts about each place in the space provided.

Physical Features
1. Arabian Peninsula

2. Arabian Sea

3. Atlantic Ocean

4. Atlas Mountains

5. Black Sea

6. Blue Nile

7. Caspian Sea

8. Dead Sea

9. Euphrates River

10. Fertile Crescent

11. Gulf of Aden

12. Jordan River

13. Libyan Desert

14. Mediterranean Sea

15. Mt. Ararat

16. Nile River

17. Persian Gulf

18. Red Sea

19. Rub'al Khali

20. the Sahara

21. Tigris River

22. White Nile

23. Zagros Mountains

Regions/Countries/States/Provinces
24. Algeria

25. Bahrain

26. Egypt

27. Gaza Strip

28. Golan Heights

29. Iran

30. Iraq

31. Israel

32. Jordan

33. Kuwait

34. Lebanon

35. Libya

36. Morocco

37. Oman

38. Occupied Palestinian Territories

39. Qatar

40. Saudi Arabia

41. Sinai

42. Sudan

43. Syria

44. Tunisia

45. Turkey

46. United Arab Emirates

47. West Bank

48. Western Sahara

49. Yemen

Cities/Urban Areas
50. Abu Dhabi

51. Algiers

52. Amman

53. Ankara

54. Baghdad

55. Beirut

56. Cairo

57. Damascus

58. Doha

59. Gaza

60. Jerusalem

61. Khartoum

62. Kuwait

63. Makkah (Mecca)

64. Manamah

65. Muscat

66. Rabat

67. Riyadh

68. Sana'a

69. Tehran

70. Tripoli

71. Tunis

MAPPING EXERCISES

The following mapping exercises are designed to improve your knowledge of the location of places, underscore why they are important, and clarify how they relate to one another. Some questions will ask you to locate places, compare maps, or fill in data; others will test your understanding of *why* you were asked to map the features that you did. Use the blank outline maps at the end of the chapter to complete these exercises. Additional blank outline maps can be found on the textbook's Web site: www.whfreeman.com/pulsipher5e.

1. Urbanization, female literacy, and opportunities for women

Rural women are often less secluded because they have many tasks to perform outside the home. However, women tend to have more education and job opportunities in urban areas.

- From the map of urban population (Photo Essay 6.5), shade countries from light to dark that have the following percent of urbanization: 0-39%; 40-59%; 60-79%; and 80-100%.
- Using the maps of human well-being (Figure 6.19), use a graduated symbol (e.g., from small to large circles) to represent the "female earned income as a % of male income" for all the countries in the region.
- Inside each country's boundary, write in the percentage of women over age 14 who produced goods and services in the formal economy (Figure 6.17).
- You will also need to refer to the map of restrictions placed on women (Figure 6.14).

Questions

    a. What relationship would you expect between a country's urbanization and: 1) the number of women who are working in the formal economy, and 2) the restrictions placed on women? Why would you expect these relationships? Where do you see them?

    b. What relationship would you expect to see between female earned income as a percent of male income and the restrictions placed on women? Where do you see these relationships?

   c. Choose two countries that stand out as contradictory to what you would expect. Explain why this might be the case for each country.

2. Oil wealth and human well-being

Oil wealth in the region is not evenly distributed. Many live in poverty with a less than desirable quality of life, while a few are extremely wealthy.

- Shade each country in the region according to its GDP per capita (Figure 6.19). Use the following categories: $0-1999; $2000-9999, $10,000-29,999, and $30,000 or more.
- Using Figure 6.20 (map of economic issues), as accurately as possible, shade the specific oil- and gas-producing areas.
- Also using Figure 6.20, cross-hatch (///) the countries that are OPEC members.
- Finally, write L (for very low or low), M (for medium-low, medium, or medium-high), or H (for high or very high) for the HDI ranking for all countries in the region (Figure 6.19).

Questions

   a. List the countries that have oil and gas production. What is the general relationship between GDP per capita and oil and gas production? Are there any anomalies? If so, explain why.

   b. For each oil- and gas-producing country, compare its GDP per capita to its HDI. Overall, in countries where GDP per capita is high, does HDI also rank high? Is it what you expected? Why or why not?

   c. Overall, how is oil *positively* affecting the region's people, the economy, and politics? How is it *negatively* affecting the region's people, the economy, and politics?

3. The importance of (clean) water

Most people in this region understand the importance, even the necessity, of living near sources of water; thus, it is vital that these water sources are clean.

- Use Figure 6.5 (global freshwater availability and stress) to shade those countries with only 0-1700 cubic meters of water per person.
- Using the population density map (Photo Essay 6.4) shade the areas that have more than 1300 people per square mile (more than 500 people per square kilometer).
- Finally, use a hatch pattern (///) to indicate those areas with high or extreme vulnerability to climate change (Photo Essay 6.3).

Questions

   b. Given the current population distribution and the availability of freshwater, where do you think the region's rapidly increasing numbers of people will live? Next, compare the map you made with the map of human impact (Figure 6.35). Based on where you predicted the growing population would live, how might this growth be problematic? How might it further increase water shortages and desertification?

    c. Compare the map you made with agricultural zones and irrigation areas in the Arabian Peninsula (Figure 6.6). Discuss (and explain) what you think the future holds for one of the countries featured on this map.

    d. Finally, compare the map you made with Figure 6.7 (dams on the Tigris and Euphrates) and discuss (and explain) what you think the future holds for Turkey and Iraq's water supply.

SAMPLE EXAM QUESTIONS

The following are sample questions to help you review for an exam. Answers are found in the back of this study guide.

1. Which statement best describes the governments in North Africa and Southwest Asia today?
a) They are democratic and representational.
b) At least half of their leaders are women.
c) They encourage complete freedom of the press.
d) They have parliaments and elections, but the parliaments have limited powers.

2. What is happening to the water supply of North Africa and Southwest Asia?
a) It is declining, mostly due to evaporation.
b) It is declining, mostly due to population growth and new modern uses.
c) It is increasing, as the deserts recede.
d) It is increasing, due to population decline and water rationing.

3. Which of the following is not a possible consequence of climate change in North Africa and Southwest Asia?
a) a rise in sea level affecting the Nile Delta and its people
b) reduced water availability and food security
c) intense rainfall and flooding
d) easier extraction of oil

4. The zone in North Africa and Southwest Asia known for its plentiful fresh water, open grasslands, and abundant wild grains is:
a) the Fertile Crescent.
b) Mesopotamia.
c) Ur.
d) the Rub'al Khali.

5. Which of the following statements describes the relationship between agriculture and gender roles in ancient North Africa and Southwest Asia?
a) The development of agriculture may have led to markedly distinct roles for men and women.

b) The roles played by men and women in hunting-gathering societies remain intact as societies became more agricultural.

c) In pre-agricultural societies, men had more status than women.

d) Inheritance lines and lineage were more important in hunting-gathering societies than in settled agricultural societies.

6. Which statement is not true regarding the lives of children in North Africa and Southwest Asia?

a) In most families, whether urban or rural, children contribute to the family's welfare from a very young age.

b) The lives of children take place overwhelmingly within the family compound or adjacent family apartments.

c) In most parts of North Africa and Southwest Asia, a much larger percentage of boys than girls go to school.

d) School, television, and the Internet are increasingly broadening the lives of this region's children.

7. The current era of price fluctuations in gas and oil began when:

a) the United States stopped supporting governments in the North Africa and Southwest Asia region.

b) Japan brought the United States into World War II by bombing Pearl Harbor.

c) the countries of North Africa and Southwest Asia nationalized the oil industry.

d) the United Nations instituted a policy to pay the countries of North Africa and Southwest Asia a higher price for their oil.

8. Which of the following is a critique of global culture held by many Muslims?

a) It leads to the erosion of traditional values.

b) It involves technology that is outlawed by traditional Islam.

c) It promotes the community interest over that of the individual.

d) It promotes Christianity over all other religions.

9. Given the nature of gender roles in urban Islamic culture, in which of the following activities would a man be least likely involved?

a) obtaining water and fuel wood for domestic use

b) managing a local business

c) receiving training at technical school

d) working as a government official

10. Which of the following is NOT among the Five Pillars of Islamic Practice?

a) seclusion of women

b) pilgrimage to the Islamic holy places

c) obligatory almsgiving (2 to 3 percent of one's income)

d) daily prayer at one or more of five times during the day

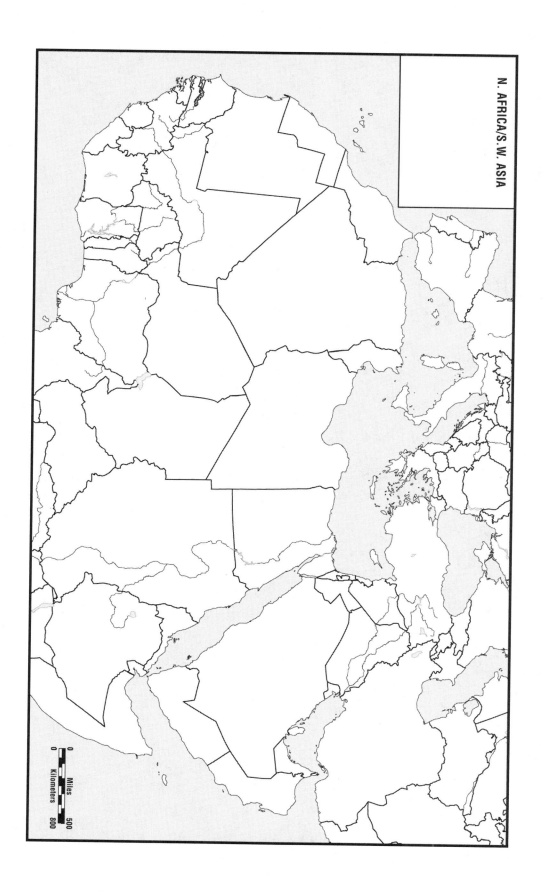

Miles

Kilometers

0

0

500

800

North Africa and Southwest Asia

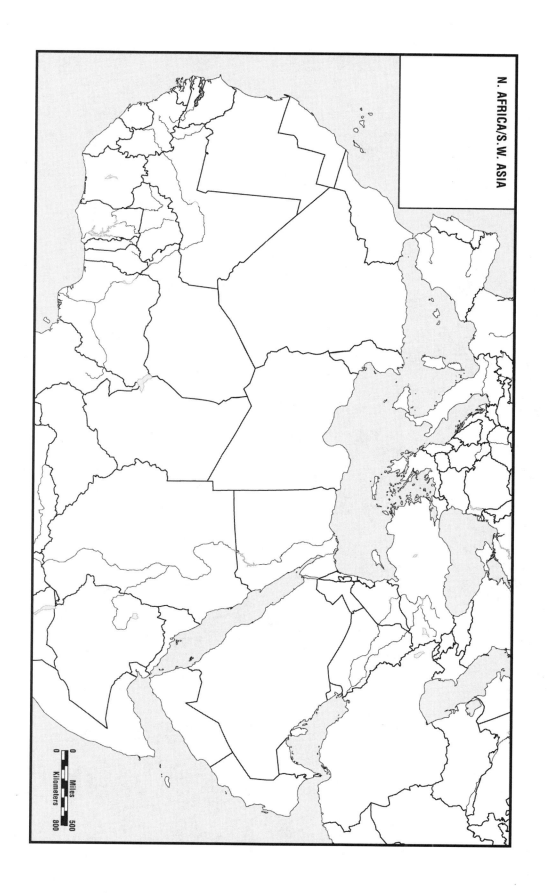

Miles

Kilometers

0
0

500
800

North Africa and Southwest Asia

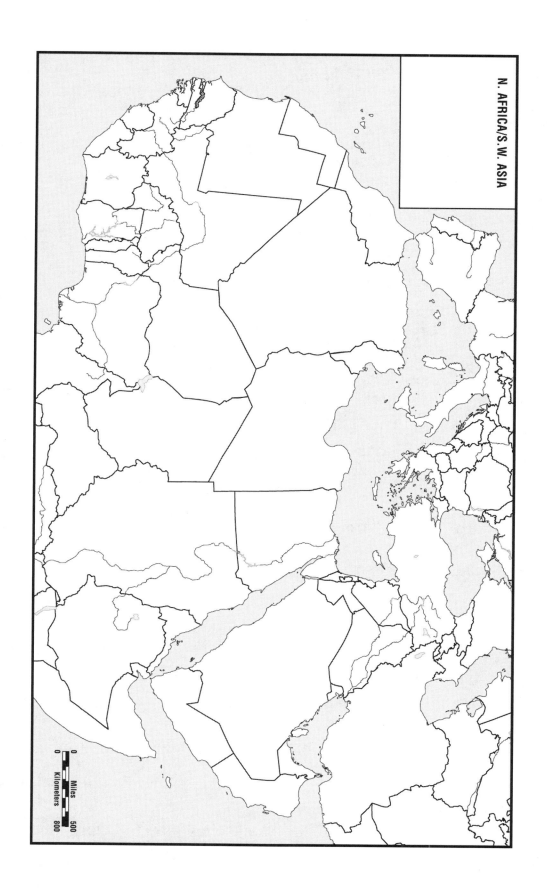

0
0
Miles
Kilometers
500
800

North Africa and Southwest Asia

CHAPTER SEVEN
Sub-Saharan Africa

LEARNING OBJECTIVES
After reading the chapter and working through this study guide, you should understand how the textbook's nine thematic concepts relate to sub-Saharan Africa.

- Climate change: Know how landforms and climate have challenged human beings and hindered Africa's development and connection to the outside world. Understand why this region is particularly vulnerable to climate change and the effects it is having on people and the environment.
- Democratization: Understand why true independence from colonial domination is so difficult to achieve. Based on the region's mixed results in democratization, understand the factors that lead to successful and responsive democracies.
- Development: Know the reasons for economic struggles and resource dependency in sub-Saharan Africa. Know what global, regional, and local measures are being taken or considered to achieve economic sustainability and subsequent improvements in human well-being.
- Food: Understand how and why agricultural systems are changing in the region. Also understand how different food production systems are helping the region adapt to climate change.
- Gender: Know how colonization and the introduction of new religions have affected gender roles. Also understand the realities of women's lives as farmers, child bearers, food producers, informal sector workers in the markets, etc.
- Globalization: Know how outsiders, including colonizers, have influenced the region and understand the consequences of their actions. Understand how Asian countries are today influencing sub-Saharan Africa's position in the global economy.
- Population: Understand why Africa's population is growing so rapidly, the consequences of this growth, and what it would take for it to be reduced. Also understand why diseases, including HIV-AIDS, are spreading so rapidly and are so difficult to control. Know the effects of these diseases on the population and on society.
- Urbanization: Understand why cities are growing so rapidly, and the effects urbanization has on fertility, living conditions, health, and employment. Also understand the effects that growth has on the formation, growth, and persistence of slums.
- Water: Know the ways in which the leading environmental problems in this region – desertification, deforestation, diminishing wildlife, and water scarcity – are being addressed in the context of current economic and political challenges. Also understand how humans have contributed to these problems.

KEY TERMS

The following terms are in **bold** in the textbook. Page numbers for each term can be found in the Chapter Key Terms list at the end of the textbook chapter. In the space next to the term (or on a separate sheet or flash cards), you can fill in the definitions for reference or quiz yourself for exam review. Definitions are found in the glossary of the textbook, as well as in the sidebars on the page they first appear.

agroforestry

animism

apartheid

carbon sequestration

civil society

commodities

currency devaluation

desertification

divide and rule

dual economy

female genital mutilation (FGM)

genocide

grassroots economic development

Horn of Africa

informal economy

intertropical convergence zone (ITCZ)

lingua franca

mixed agriculture

pastoralism

polygyny

Sahel

self-reliant development

shifting cultivation

subsistence agriculture

REVIEW QUESTIONS

The following review questions are related directly to the textbook material. These questions can be used to help you prepare for an exam, or you may want to read through the questions before you begin reading the textbook, quizzing yourself after you complete each section.

The Geographic Setting

1. Why are Africa's landforms so exceptionally uniform? What effect has this had on transportation and trade?

2. What are the general characteristics of Africa's climates? What effect does the ITCZ have on climate? What challenges do these climates bring to human beings?

3. What are some causes and possible outcomes of deforestation? How might deforestation be slowed or halted in this region?

4. What are the benefits and drawbacks of subsistence agriculture, mixed agriculture, and commercial agriculture? How is climate change affecting water management for agriculture in the region?

5. In what ways is Africa the home of humans, as well as early agriculture, industry, and trade? Why is this rich past often misunderstood?

6. What were some of the causes and negative outcomes of internal and external slavery in Africa?

7. Why did European powers establish colonies in this region? What were the effects of colonization on human well-being, agriculture, politics, population, and the economy? What are some of the lingering problems with the boundaries that colonizers drew?

8. What is apartheid and what was its purpose? What was the role of the Boers? Even though apartheid has ended in South Africa, what are some lingering after-effects that are especially pernicious?

Current Geographic Issues

9. Why are raw materials/commodities an unstable base for the economy, and why is it difficult to reduce this dependency? How is South Africa an exception to commodity dependence?

10. Why are some African countries enacting structural adjustment programs (SAPs)? What are some of the benefits and drawbacks of SAPs in this region?

11. With formal sector employment difficult to find, many people are becoming involved in the informal economy. What are the benefits and drawbacks?

12. How is globalization, particularly investment and trade with Asia, changing this region's position in the global economy? What are the effects of China and India's influence in the region?

13. What are the benefits and limitations of regional economic integration and grassroots rural economic development?

14. Why are politics and ethnicity so problematic in this region? How has conflict been exacerbated by resources, the Cold War, and refugees? Why is democracy so hard to achieve in Africa? What are some signs that democracy is on the rise?

15. How is population density in the region misleading? How does the rapid population growth of this region affect standards of living? Why are Africans still having large families? What are some factors that might cause growth rates to decline?

16. Although most people live in villages, mass migration to cities is occurring. Why is this the case, and what is the effect of rapid urbanization on large cities and their infrastructure?

17. How might the HIV-AIDS epidemic affect population growth and life expectancy? Why is HIV-AIDS more difficult to control in Africa than in other, wealthier regions? What are some of the factors contributing to its rapid spread? What are some of the social consequences of this problem?

18. Considering GDP, HDI rankings, and F/EIM, what is the overall status of human well-being in this region? What are some of the reasons for these rankings?

19. What are the general characteristics of gender roles in this region? What are the origins of these roles and how are these roles changing?

20. What are the common characteristics of indigenous belief systems? How did Islam and Christianity spread to this part of the world?

CRITICAL THINKING EXERCISES

The following questions ask you to apply the ideas and principles you learned from the textbook to new situations.

1. Misunderstandings and biased views

It is impossible to generalize about sub-Saharan African countries because environments, political systems, and ethnic groups are so diverse; thus, it is often the subject of misrepresentation and unwarranted, often negative, generalizations. The language used to describe Africa has been particularly prone to ethnocentrism.

- Before you start reading the textbook for this region, write down ten characteristics (generalizations) about it.
- After you've read the chapter and discussed it in class, look at your list again. Would you consider any of the terms you used to be ethnocentric? Why do you think this is the case? Have these views changed after reading the chapter?

2. Apartheid

Apartheid laws were enacted in 1948 to reinforce the long-standing segregation in South Africa. Everyone except whites had to carry passbooks and live in racially segregated areas or homelands. The fight to end racial discrimination in South Africa actually began before apartheid laws were even introduced. When apartheid finally ended, one of the most prominent resisters of apartheid was elected president.

- Consider the historical and current relationships that Caucasians have with African Americans, Hispanic Americans, Asian Americans, and Native Americans in the United States. How are these situations similar to apartheid in South Africa?
- How have race relations changed in the United States since the official end of segregation in the 1960s? How have they changed in South Africa since the end of apartheid? Be sure to consider the fact that laws may have changed, but there is a lag time in how people's attitudes and actions change.
- Do you think South Africa should use the United States as a model for desegregation efforts? Why or why not?

3. Africa's importance in the global economy

Africa is often assumed to be unimportant to the global economy because it is poor and makes only a small contribution to the world's commerce. However, Africa is actually inextricably linked to the global economy because of its reliance on exports and imports.

- Do you think Africa plays a unique role in the global economy? Why or why not?
- Consider the objects in your room/apartment/house. What products do you think might be made from African raw materials?
- Using the textbook, Internet, or other sources, identify at least ten of Africa's main exports. Are you surprised? Why or why not? Start with the following Web sites:
  - www.cia.gov/cia/publications/factbook
  - reportweb.usitc.gov/africa/trade_data.jsp
- With this knowledge, reconsider what objects in your room/apartment/house could be from Africa. Keep in mind that you may not have many *finished* products from Africa, but many things you own might be made from Africa's raw materials. List at least ten things that are or could be made from African materials.
- After completing this exercise, reassess your first answer: Do you think Africa plays a unique role in the global economy? Why or why not?

4. Settlement patterns

Human settlements take many forms and the various types of living arrangements reflect how people relate to one another economically, politically, and socially. By 2030, it is estimated that the urban population in the region will double.

- Make a list of the positive and negative aspects of living in rural and urban areas in your own country. Consider economic, political, and social characteristics. What are some of the differences between living in rural and urban areas in your country compared to rural and urban areas in a sub-Saharan African country?
- Would you choose to live in an urban or rural setting in your country? How about in sub-Saharan Africa? Are your reasons because of push factors or pull factors?

5. Female genital mutilation

Multiple and complex symbolic meanings explain this deeply ingrained custom. Although many see it as an extreme human rights abuse, it has significant importance to others.

- Why is female genital mutilation (FGM) so important and ingrained in certain value systems? What are some arguments defenders of this practice make to support it?
- What are some of the negative consequences?
- Would this custom be acceptable in the United States? Why or why not? Do you think it is practiced in the United States? Using the Internet or other resources, find out if it is practiced in the United States.
- Does the United States have any similar rituals?
- Should the practice of FGM end? Defend your response. If you answered yes, what can be done to eliminate FGM?

IMPORTANT PLACES

The following places are featured in the chapter. Make sure you can locate all of them on a map. Blank outline maps can be found on the textbook's Web site: www.whfreeman.com/pulsipher5e. Also, to prepare for quizzes and exams, write a few important facts about each place in the space provided.

Physical Features

1. Atlantic Ocean

2. Cape of Good Hope

3. Congo Basin

4. Congo (Zaire) River

5. Ethiopian Highlands

6. Great Rift Valley

7.   Gulf of Guinea

8.   Horn of Africa

9.   Indian Ocean

10.   Kalahari Desert

11.   Katanga Plateau

12.   Lake Chad

13.   Lake Kariba

14.   Lake Malawi

15.   Lake Tanganyika

16.   Lake Victoria

17.   Lake Volta

18.   Mount Kenya

19.   Mount Kilimanjaro

20.   Mozambique Channel

21.   Namib Desert

22.   Niger River

23.   Orange River

24.   the Sahara

25.   Sahel

26.   Somali Peninsula

27.   Victoria Falls

28.   Zambezi River

Regions/Countries/States/Provinces

29.   Angola

30.   Benin

31.   Botswana

32.   Burkina Faso

33.   Burundi

34.   Cameroon

35.   Cape Verde

36.   Central African Republic

37.   Chad

38.   Comoros

39.   Côte d'Ivoire

40.   Democratic Republic of the Congo (Kinshasa)

41.   Djibouti

42.   Equatorial Guinea

43.   Eritrea

44.   Ethiopia

45.   Gabon

46.   The Gambia

47.   Ghana

48.   Guinea

49.   Guinea-Bissau

50.   Kenya

51. Lesotho

52. Liberia

53. Madagascar

54. Malawi

55. Mali

56. Mauritania

57. Mauritius

58. Mozambique

59. Namibia

60. Niger

61. Nigeria

62. Ogoniland

63. Republic of Congo (Brazzaville)

64. Réunion

65. Rwanda

66. São Tomé and Príncipe

67. Senegal

68. Seychelles

69. Sierra Leone

70. Somalia

71. South Africa

72. Swaziland

73. Tanzania

74. Togo

75. Uganda

76. Zambia

77. Zimbabwe

Cities/Urban Areas

78. Abuja

79. Accra

80. Addis Ababa

81. Antananarivo

82. Asmera

83. Bamako

84. Bangui

85. Banjul

86. Bissau

87. Brazzaville

88. Bujumbura

89. Cape Town

90. Conakry

91. Dakar

92. Dar es Salaam

93. Djibouti

94. Freetown

95. Gaborone

96. Harare

97. Kampala

98. Kigali

99. Kinshasa

100. Libreville

101. Lilongwe

102. Lomé

103. Luanda

104. Lusaka

105. Malabo

106. Maputo

107. Maseru

108. Mbabane

109. Mogadishu

110. Monrovia

111. Moroni

112. Nairobi

113. N'Djamena

114. Niamey

115. Nouakchott

116.   Ouagadougou

117.   Port Louis

118.   Porto Novo

119.   Praia

120.   Pretoria

121.   São Tomé

122.   Victoria

123.   Windhoek

124.   Yamoussoukro

125.   Yaoundé

MAPPING EXERCISES

The following mapping exercises are designed to improve your knowledge of the location of places, underscore why they are important, and clarify how they relate to one another. Some questions will ask you to locate places, compare maps, or fill in data; others will test your understanding of *why* you were asked to map the features that you did. Use the blank outline maps at the end of the chapter to complete these exercises. Additional blank outline maps can be found on the textbook's Web site: www.whfreeman.com/pulsipher5e.

1. Population growth, education, and HIV-AIDS

HIV-AIDS is the most severe public health problem in sub-Saharan Africa. It is having dramatic effects on population growth and life expectancy patterns. However, education is beginning to play a changing role in the spread and control of HIV-AIDS.

- Shade those countries that have 5 percent or more of adults with HIV-AIDS. Use the categories that are presented in Figure 7.25. Label these countries.
- From the current year's "World Population Data Sheet," found at www.prb.org, look up the countries you labeled. Draw a hatch pattern over the countries that have over 2 percent rate of natural increase.
- Also from the World Population Data Sheet, use a graduated symbol (e.g., from small to large circles), and draw a symbol in each of these countries to illustrate the percent of married women using all methods of contraception.

Questions

    a. What is the current relationship between HIV-AIDS and population rate of natural increase? Explain why this is the case.

    b. If the situation stays the same, how will HIV-AIDS affect life expectancy and population growth of this region 20 years from now? How could this situation be changed?

    c. Which of these countries do you think will experience the greatest *decrease* in population growth rate? Why?

    d. Examining the contraception data, how might increased education affect countries that have high HIV-AIDS rates? How will it affect those with high growth rates? Explain why. Some countries with high HIV-AIDS rates *do* have relatively high rates (more than 50 percent) of contraception use; why do you think they still have high rates of HIV-AIDS? How can education be improved in a population with such high rates of HIV-AIDS, when many parents are unable to pay for school fees?

2. Democracy and the provision of basic needs

In examining the daily suffering of many Africans, many wonder if African governments should meet their citizens' basic needs for food, shelter, and health care *before* they open up to a democratic form of government.

- Using Photo Essay 7.4, use three different colors to shade the countries that are full democracy, flawed democracy, and hybrid regime. Label all the countries you shaded.
- Use graduated symbols (e.g., from small to large triangles) to illustrate the Human Development Index (Figure 7.27).

Questions

    a. Based on your map, what type of government meets basic needs better? Why do you think this is the case?

    b. In light of the suffering of Africa's people, explain whether you think African governments should meet basic needs like food, shelter, and health care before they focus on achieving democracy.

    c. Consider some of the difficulties governments face in providing for citizens:

       - How can countries provide for needs when they have a very limited tax base from which to draw?

       - Many of these countries were established as democracies at independence, yet authoritarian presidents have caused major problems. How do you make a corrupt dictator take care of the basic needs of the people?

    d. Explain if you think Africa would be better off left alone, or should other countries help provide basic needs for Africans?

3. The limits on carrying capacity

Carrying capacity depends on physical factors, including water supply and quality, soil condition, and disease, as well as cultural, social, economic, and political factors, including agriculture, wealth, and political unrest.

- Shade (in yellow) the countries with 5 percent or more of their population infected with HIV-AIDS (Figure 7.25).
- Choose a symbol to draw in each country with GDP per capita less than $1000 (Figure 7.27).
- Place a symbol in each country that has experienced armed conflicts and genocides with over 180,000 deaths since 1945 (Photo Essay 7.4).
- Using the regional map of sub-Saharan Africa (Figure 7.1), outline (in light brown) and label the Kalahari and Namib Deserts, and the Sahara.
- Also using Figure 7.1, trace and label the major rivers in the region with a heavy blue line: Niger, Orange, Congo (Zaire), Nile, White Nile, Blue Nile, and Zambezi.
- Using the map of human impact (Photo Essay 7.2), shade areas that have high impact and medium-high impact on the land.

<u>Questions</u>

 a. Make a list of five countries on your map that appear to have the potential for high carrying capacity (i.e., low human impact on the land, access to water, low HIV-AIDS rates, relative peace, and a relatively high GDP per capita).

  - From the current year's "World Population Data Sheet," found at www.prb.org, add their rate of natural increase to your list.
  - Is rapid population growth occurring? What implications might this population change have on these countries?

 b. Next, from the "World Population Data Sheet," make a list of the ten fastest growing countries in sub-Saharan Africa (based on rate of natural increase). Label these ten countries on your map.

  - Examining your map, does the carrying capacity of each of these ten rapidly growing countries appear to be high or low? Write high or low next to each.
  - What implications might this rapid growth have on the countries that already have a low carrying capacity?

SAMPLE EXAM QUESTIONS

The following are sample questions to help you review for an exam. Answers are found in the back of this study guide.

1. Which of the following is the most accurate general description of the geomorphology of the African continent?
a) It resembles a dinner plate with a sunken interior ringed by weathered mountains.
b) It is comparable to a rumpled carpet with high mountains and narrow valleys.
c) It appears as an inclined plane, sloping from north to south.
d) It resembles a raised platform edged by narrow coastlines.

2. Which of the following is not part of the current efforts to reduce deforestation in Africa?
a) new laws prohibiting Asian and European companies from establishing logging companies in Africa
b) laws requiring logging companies to use methods that reduce damage from logging
c) building fewer logging roads
d) preventing poor farmers from moving into deforested areas

3. Which is not an agricultural issue currently facing Africa?
a) Some of the most common commercial crops are less well adapted to environments outside their natural range.
b) Commercial crops tend to be planted in large fields of just one crop, which leaves them vulnerable to pests.
c) The prices of commercial crops are set on the world market, which can lead to price fluctuations that leave people without enough income to survive.
d) The most common commercial crops grown in Africa are in less demand on world markets as a result of the explosion of soybean as a food staple across the world.

4. Which of the following is NOT among the general issues concerning water in sub-Saharan Africa?
a) Water must almost always be carried from a source external to the home.
b) Women procure virtually all water consumed by households.
c) Plumbing and sewage treatment are usually not available.
d) Development has increased per capita supplies of water.

5. Which of the following is not part of the PRSPs that have replaced SAPs in Africa?
a) They focus on poverty reduction rather than just development.
b) They promote participation in civil society.
c) The aim to reduce the role of government in the economy.
d) They require nations to pay back all their debt as a condition of participation.

6. Some Africans praise Chinese investment in Africa because:
a) Chinese investment usually comes with few or no demands regarding human rights or environmental stability.
b) the long Chinese colonial heritage in Africa has led to a large Chinese population on the African continent.
c) the Chinese have stricter rules regarding employment practices than the United States or Europe.
d) the currency of most African nations is pegged to the Chinese yuan.

7. By which of the following means are many of the local transport needs for the village and domestic units in sub-Saharan Africa satisfied?
a) women in animal-powered vehicles
b) women on foot
c) children on bicycles
d) men in motor vehicles

8. Among the following, which is the most obvious European legacy at the root of many armed conflicts in sub-Saharan Africa?
a) national borders
b) ethnic discrimination
c) environmental destruction
d) socialist values

9. Which statement is not true of the refugee situation in Africa?
a) Refugees are often trying to escape genocide.
b) The burden of hosting refugees can be severe for the host countries.
c) Large portions of economic aid to Africa have been diverted to meet the emergency needs of refugees.
d) Refugees are usually migrants who have moved from their home country to another country in search of work.

10. The greatest contributor to the rapid growth of cities in sub-Saharan Africa is:
a) the high birth rate.
b) the low mortality rate.
c) migration.
d) global climate change.

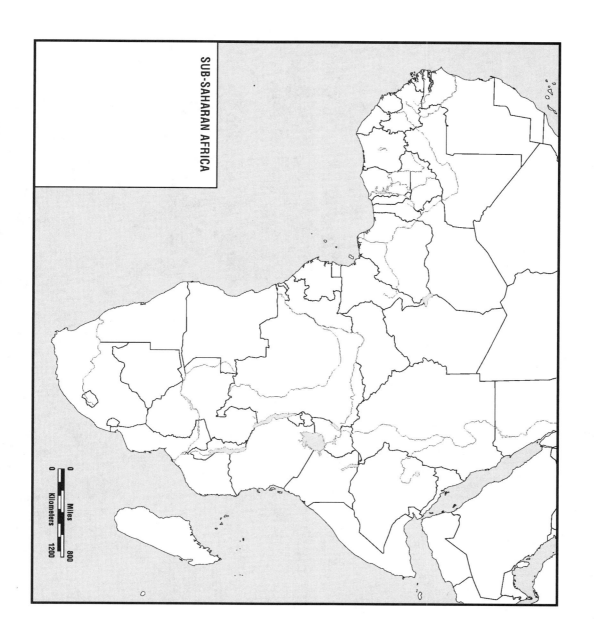

SUB-SAHARAN AFRICA

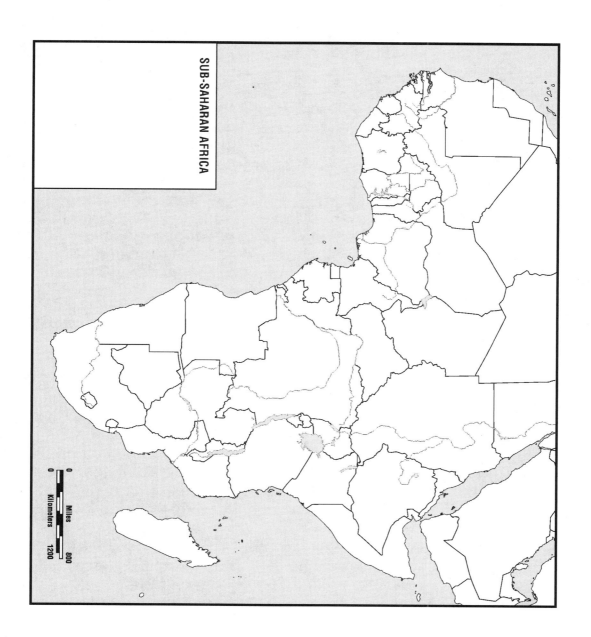

SUB-SAHARAN AFRICA

0
0
Miles
Kilometers
800
1200

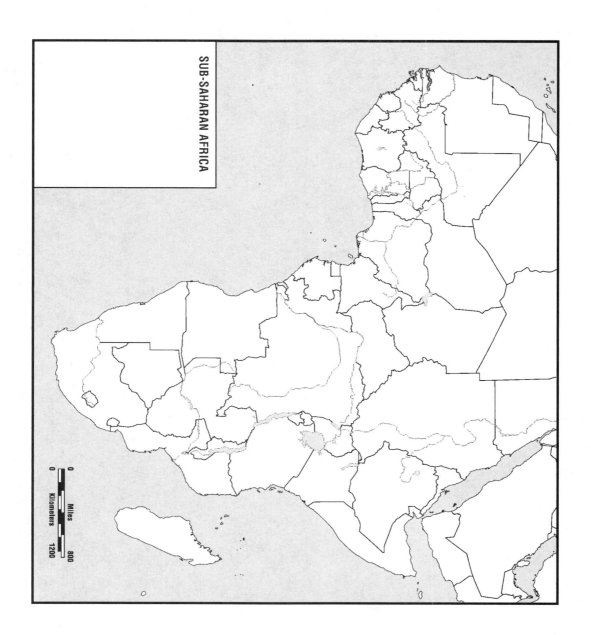

SUB-SAHARAN AFRICA

0
Miles
0
Kilometers
800
1200

CHAPTER EIGHT
South Asia

LEARNING OBJECTIVES

After reading the chapter and working through this study guide, you should understand how the textbook's nine thematic concepts relate to South Asia.

- Climate change: Understand some of the environmental issues facing South Asia and why they are so difficult to resolve. Know why this region is particularly vulnerable to climate change and what its potential effects are.
- Democratization: Be able to identify the residual positive and negative influences of British colonization and subsequent independence. Also understand why, although parts of South Asia are often praised as bastions of democracy, the region still has many tensions and potential for conflict.
- Development: Understand why this region has such startling economic incongruities. Also understand how benefits of development are distributed across various scales in this region.
- Food: Understand why the concept of virtual water is useful in assessing the sustainability of water resources in this region. Understand how changes in the region's food production systems are contributing to urbanization.
- Gender: Know the overall status of women and the effects on quality of life. Know why purdah is desired by some and not by others. Know how freeing women from purdah will affect them, their families, and their communities.
- Globalization: Know why globalization is on the rise in this region. Also understand how offshore outsourcing is benefiting the manufacturing sector.
- Population: Know why population is growing rapidly, and understand the potential consequences of such rapid growth. Know what can be, and has been, done to curtail this growth and increase quality of life.
- Urbanization: Know the reasons for the rapid growth of the region's cities. Understand the conditions migrants find themselves in when they move to these cities.
- Water: Understand how monsoon rains affect agriculture, the economy, health, and daily life. Also understand why there are conflicts over, and shortages of, water.

KEY TERMS

The following terms are in **bold** in the textbook. Page numbers for each term can be found in the Chapter Key Terms list at the end of the textbook chapter. In the space next to the term (or on a separate sheet or flash cards), you can fill in the definitions for reference or quiz yourself for exam review. Definitions are found in the glossary of the textbook, as well as in the sidebars on the page they first appear.

agroecology

Buddhism

caste system

civil disobedience

communal conflict

dowry

green revolution

Harappa culture

Hinduism

Indus Valley civilization

Jainism

jati

microcredit

monsoon

Mughals

offshore outsourcing

Partition

purdah

regional conflict

religious nationalism

Sikhism

subcontinent

Taliban

varna

REVIEW QUESTIONS

The following review questions are related directly to the textbook material. These questions can be used to help you prepare for an exam, or you may want to read through the questions before you begin reading the textbook, quizzing yourself after you complete each section.

The Geographic Setting

1. Describe the resulting landscape from the collision of tectonic plates on this region.
2. Describe the role the intertropical convergence zone (ITCZ) and monsoons play in the climate of this region. What are the consequences of such severe weather on the landscape and people?
3. Why is this region vulnerable to climate change? What are the effects of sea level rise, and what might be some outcomes and responses to climate change?
4. Why has deforestation become an issue for both urban and rural areas? Who is losing and who is benefiting from the deforestation?
5. What are some of the controversial water issues in this region? Why are they so difficult to solve? How are the poor, in particular, affected by these problems?
6. Trace the path of colonization in this region. What are some of the positive and negative legacies of the Indo-Europeans, Mughals, and the British?
7. Why was India partitioned in 1947 and what were some of the outcomes? What were the results of the civil war in Pakistan in 1971? What are relations between India and Pakistan like today?

Current Geographic Issues

8. Consider how village life and city life differ by listing the benefits and drawbacks of living in each place.
9. What are some of the roots of the great degree of ethnic and linguistic diversity?
10. What is the caste system? What activities does it affect? What are the reasons for its endurance in some areas and decline in others? What are some of the positive and negative effects it has had on societies?

11. Why is the relationship between Hindus and Muslims so complex? How do relationships differ in rural and urban areas?

12. Explain the general status of women in South Asia. Who does and does not observe purdah? How and why is this changing? How do gender roles vary from urban to rural areas, or among different religions?

13. What are some of the negative effects of the high densities and growing population on both rural and urban areas? How is this region's growing population affecting quality of life? Why does population continue to grow in this region, and what will it take to slow this growth?

14. How do South Asians survive with such low GDP per capita? What are some of the reasons why HDI rankings are so low?

15. What is the cause of the startling economic contrasts in this region? What are the effects?

16. Give at least five general characteristics of agriculture in this region. Why was the green revolution seen as a necessity? What were its positive and negative outcomes?

17. Explain microcredit. How does it work and what are the benefits to village and rural women in particular?

18. What sector(s) of the economy is/are contributing to economic globalization in this region? Why is the government focusing on industry over agriculture? What are the reasons for both the fear of and desire for globalization in this region?

19. Religious nationalism and regional conflicts are detrimental to the stability of the region. Why are they currently on the rise?

20. What are some signs that democracy is on the rise in this region?

CRITICAL THINKING EXERCISES

The following questions ask you to apply the ideas and principles you learned from the textbook to new situations.

1. Coping with monsoon rains

The seasonality of monsoons and the amount of rainfall from them dictate the lives of many people in South Asia.

- From the Web site www.worldclimate.com, find the seasonality of rains in your area and the amount of rainfall it receives (choose the nearest city if your city does not have data).
- How does the *seasonality* in your area compare with monsoon seasons in South Asia? What if you experienced the drastic seasonality experienced in parts of South Asia? How would you cope (think about agriculture, transportation, economy, daily life, etc.)?
- How does the *rainfall amount* in your area compare with the amount in places in South Asia? Collect data for several cities in South Asia that are affected by monsoon rains. Consider how this much precipitation would affect you and the area in which you live.

- Would you have to make changes in your lifestyle? What kind of changes?
- Are we in the industrialized world (with solid structures and early warning systems) so removed from climatic anomalies that rainfall amount wouldn't really matter? Justify your response.

2. Sea level rise

Millions of people in this region live near sea level, making this region quite vulnerable to climate change and the potential rise in sea level.

- Conduct some Internet research on the predicted rise in sea level in this region, paying specific attention to recent reports regarding the number of people and amount of land that might be affected. You may be surprised at the shocking statistics that have been presented lately.
- After reading a number of reports and news articles, summarize the potential effects that even a small rise in sea level can have. Consider effects on people, land, architecture and cities, historic sites and artifacts, the fishing industry, and more.
- Consider what these displaced people will do, and where they will go. How will a rise in sea level indirectly impact other surrounding areas (consider migration, pressure on food supplies, infrastructure in cities, and more)?
- Finally, what can be done to minimize the impact of sea level rise in this region? Consider both local and international strategies, as well as both natural and man-made solutions.

3. Are there other forms of the caste system?

In South Asia, the caste system divides society into a social hierarchy. Traditionally, a person is born into a caste, which cannot be changed. It affects nearly all aspects of daily life.

- All human groups have deeply ingrained concepts of relative social status. Consider the caste system in South Asia as well as social differentiation in your own society.
    - Does the society you live in have anything that resembles the caste system (think about race, gender, age, occupation, location, etc.)? Make a list of categories in one of these "caste systems" in your society.
    - How is "caste" indicated (think about clothes, hairstyle, body decorations, manner of speaking, material possessions, space occupied, gender, religion, etc.)?
    - What "caste" would you fit into in the categories you listed?
    - What effects does this system have on your everyday life and society in general?
- Many South Asians converted from Hindu to Islam to escape life as a member of a low-status caste. Consider if you would be willing to change your belief system in order to escape the "caste" you are in. How could it be done?

4. Purdah and the status of women

Purdah is the practice of concealing women from the eyes of nonfamily men. This is a widely accepted practice in many parts of the world and has dramatic effects on women's lives and relationships.

- Why is purdah so accepted in this region? Do you think it would be acceptable in your society? Why or why not? What can you think of in your society that compares to the practice of purdah?
- How would living under purdah affect your life and the choices you make?
- Some women choose seclusion in South Asia. What reasons do they give for this choice? Under what circumstances might *you* want to practice purdah?
- What are the benefits of *ending* the practice of purdah to men, women, and children?

5. Microcredit at your fingertips

South Asians have developed innovative ways to help the poor. In 2006, Dr. Mohammed Yunus was awarded the Nobel Peace Prize for his creation the Grameen Bank in the 1970s. Not only has the Grameen Bank lent more than $8 billion to over 8 million borrowers, many other organizations, both international and local, have found success with microlending.

- Research microlending/microcredit in your local community (or the nearest large city). Were you surprised at what you found? Does a local microcredit group or national organization serve your community? What types of projects are being funded and how is repayment organized?
- Newer international microcredit organizations are also finding success. For example, Kiva, started by a young couple in San Francisco in 2004, allows people all over the world to lend in increments of $25 through PayPal. Internet technology allows you to see photos of borrowers and read their stories before selecting a loan to fund. While your borrower is working hard to get out of poverty in Tanzania, Paraguay, Azerbaijan, or elsewhere, you are continually updated as they repay their loan to your PayPal account. Research Kiva (www.kiva.org) and similar international lending institutions (start with www.slate.com/id/2161797). What types of projects are being funded and how is repayment organized?
- Do you think this is a promising strategy for helping the working poor? Does it appear to be a success? Justify your answers.

IMPORTANT PLACES

The following places are featured in the chapter. Make sure you can locate all of them on a map. Blank outline maps can be found on the textbook's Web site: www.whfreeman.com/pulsipher5e. Also, to prepare for quizzes and exams, write a few important facts about each place in the space provided.

Physical Features

1. Arabian Sea

2. Bay of Bengal

3. Brahmaputra River

4. Deccan Plateau

5. Eastern Ghats

6. Ganga (Ganges) River

7. Ganga-Brahmaputra Delta

8. Himalayas

9. Hindu Kush

10. Indian Ocean

11. Indo-Gangetic Plain

12. Indus River

13. Narmada River

14. Nilgiri Hills

15. Thar Desert

16. Western Ghats

Regions/Countries/States/Provinces

17. Afghanistan

18. Ahraura

19. Bangladesh

20. Bhutan

21. Dharavi

22. Gujarat

23. India

24. Joypur

25. Kashmir

26. Kerala

27. Maldives

28. Nepal

29. Pakistan

30. Punjab

31. Sri Lanka

Cities/Urban Areas
32. Colombo

33. Delhi/New Delhi

34. Dhaka

35. Islamabad

36. Kabul

37. Kathmandu

38. Kolkata (Calcutta)

39. Mumbai (Bombay)

40. Thimphu

MAPPING EXERCISES

The following mapping exercises are designed to improve your knowledge of the location of places, underscore why they are important, and clarify how they relate to one another. Some questions will ask you to locate places, compare maps, or fill in data; others will test your understanding of *why* you were asked to map the features that you did. Use the blank outline maps at the end of the chapter to complete these exercises. Additional blank outline maps can be found on the textbook's Web site: www.whfreeman.com/pulsipher5e.

1. Relationship between landforms and population

South Asia has some of the most spectacular landforms and important rivers on earth. Some of these physical features make the land more habitable than others. In addition, humans often manipulate the physical landscape to make it *more* habitable.

- From the map of the region (Figure 8.1), draw the outline, and label the Deccan Plateau.
- Draw (with ^^^) and label the location of these mountain ranges: Eastern Ghats, Western Ghats, Himalayas, and Hindu Kush (Figure 8.1).
- Draw a heavy blue line over these rivers: Brahmaputra, Ganga (Ganges), Indus, and Narmada (Figure 8.1). Label each of these rivers. From Figure 8.2 place a dot at the location of the Sardar Sarovar Dam.
- Shade the areas that have over 1300 persons per square mile (over 500 people per square kilometer) (Photo Essay 8.4).

Questions

a. Based on the information you mapped, is population concentrated in specific locations (i.e., coastal or interior, along rivers or mountain ranges, etc.)? If so, where?

b. What is the general relationship between population and each of the different landforms: plateaus, mountains, and rivers? Explain the reasons for each.

c. Consider the Sardar Sarovar Dam on the Narmada River. Why was it built? What are the pros and cons of building this dam?

2. How does climate affect people's lives and location?

This region has a great variety of regional climates, ranging from tropical monsoon to deserts. These physical conditions can have major impacts on living conditions. Climate change can perhaps make these impacts even greater.

- Shade in the general location of temperate climates (in green) and the arid and semiarid climates (in orange) (Photo Essay 8.1).
- Use a hatch pattern (///) to show where population density is more than 1300 persons per square mile (more than 500 people per square kilometer) (Photo Essay 8.4).
- Use the opposite hatch pattern (\\\) to show the areas with the heaviest (both winter and summer) monsoon rains (Figure 8.4).

Questions
a. Based on the information you mapped, what is the general relationship between population and each of the two climate types? Why is this the case for each?
b. Examine the areas where the hatch patterns cross (high population density *and* heavy monsoon rains). List at least three positive and three negative effects of monsoon rains on the people in these densely populated areas.
c. Compare the map you made to that of vulnerability to climate change (Photo Essay 8.2). Based on your responses to the above questions, what are some potential negative impacts of climate change in this region? What are some responses to climate change in this region?

3. Female literacy and population growth rates

The overall status of women in South Asia is low; however, their relative well-being varies geographically. Freeing women from purdah encourages lower fertility rates and allows women to improve their own educational attainment and overall well-being, as well as that of their children.

- Using Figure 8.18, shade the region's female literacy rate from light to dark using these categories: less than 35%; 35.01-65%; and 65.01% and higher.
- Referring to Figure 8.23, use a graduated symbol (e.g., from small to large circles) to map "female earned income as a % of male income."
- Finally, write in the 2009 total fertility rate for the countries provided in Figure 8.20 (decline in fertility).

Questions
a. Does population growth (total fertility rate) generally increase or decrease as education (female literacy rate) increases? Explain why you see the relationship indicated on the map. Is it what you expected?
b. Do you see any anomalies (e.g., high literacy/high growth rate or low literacy/low growth rate)? Why might this be the case for at least one country you picked out on the map?
c. Discuss how female income as a percent of male income corresponds to education (literacy rate) and population growth (total fertility rate) on your map. Discuss the future of women's employment opportunities and income based on what you see on your map.

SAMPLE EXAM QUESTIONS

The following are sample questions to help you review for an exam. Answers are found in the back of this study guide.

1. Which statement does NOT describe the cultural adjustments that rural people have to make to cope with South Asia's contrasting climatic seasons?
a) Cattle and goats become aquatic during the wet summer months.
b) Villagers fast during the dry winter months to save their food for the wet summer months.
c) Villages become self-sustaining islands during the summer months due to the monsoon rains that cut them off from civilization.
d) Villagers move their valuables into boats tied to their houses during the summer monsoons to prevent losses during flooding.

2. All of the following are efforts to respond to the threats of climate change in South Asia except:
a) development of solar and wind energy.
b) underground water management systems.
c) reduction of carbon dioxide emissions via electric (rather than gasoline-powered) cars.
d) technologies to disperse or reverse monsoon wind patterns before they reach the region.

3. Which of the following has not been an intended or unintended effect of India's diversion of the Ganga River's flow to Kolkata?
a) Channels have been flushed out where silt is accumulating and hampering river traffic.
b) The people of Bangladesh have benefited at the expense of the citizens of Kolkata.
c) Salt water from the Bay of Bengal penetrates inland, ruining agricultural fields.
d) The fishing industry in Bangladesh has been damaged.

4. Which of the following characteristics of modern South Asian governments is NOT a legacy of British colonial rule?
a) a tendency to provide tax benefits to agricultural producers rather than heavy industry
b) bureaucracies and red tape
c) resistance to change
d) a tendency to remain aloof from the people

5. Which statement is not true of Dharavi, India?
a) It is one of the world's largest shantytowns/slums.
b) It is home to many inventive entrepreneurs.
c) It is the target of real estate development projects that will displace residents.
d) Its population is not affected by global economic downturns.

6. Which of the following is not true of the caste system today?
a) There are differences in wealth among the members of any particular caste.
b) Members of a particular *jati* tend to dress in a similar manner and speak the same dialect.
c) Membership in a specific caste requires following a particular occupation.
d) Untouchables and Adivasis benefit from an affirmative action program that guarantees that a certain percentage of government jobs go to these groups.

7. Which of the following statements is NOT true in regard to the practice of purdah in South Asia?
a) It is common in places where Islam is the main religion.
b) It is typically perceived as a mark of poverty.
c) It is not observed by aboriginal groups and low-caste Hindus.
d) It discourages participation of women in public life.

8. Which of the following does NOT characterize any aspect of the green revolution in South Asia?
a) greatly boosted grain harvests
b) improved the mechanization of agriculture
c) benefits accrued to poorer farmers
d) introduced new seeds and fertilizers

9. All of the following factors are drawing foreign investment into India except:
a) the large and cheap Indian workforce.
b) the large pent-up domestic demand for manufactured goods.
c) the excellent educational infrastructure for the middle and upper classes.
d) the official government policy of employing children for lower wages than adults.

10. The terrorist attack in Mumbai in November 2008 was most likely related to:
a) Hindu/Muslim conflicts in the region.
b) the resurgence of the Tamil Tigers.
c) the Burma junta.
d) the Islamic militancy based in Afghanistan and Pakistan.

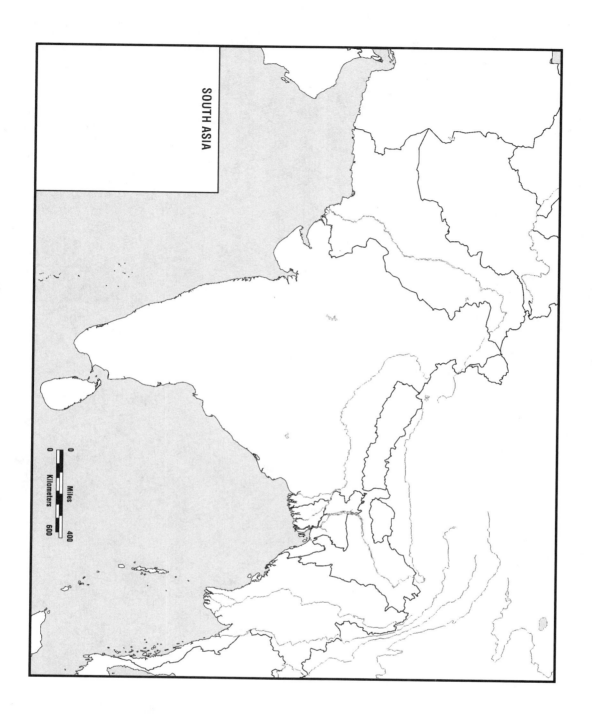

SOUTH ASIA

0
Miles
0
Kilometers
400
600

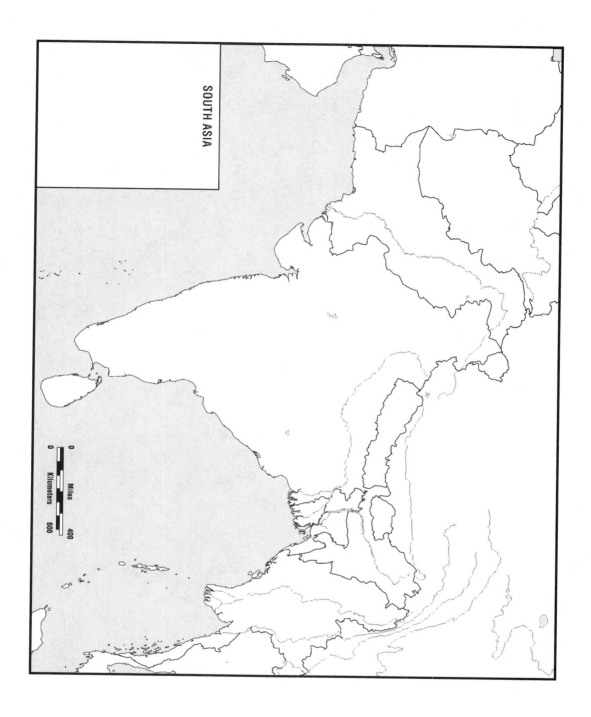

SOUTH ASIA

0 Miles 400
0 Kilometers 600

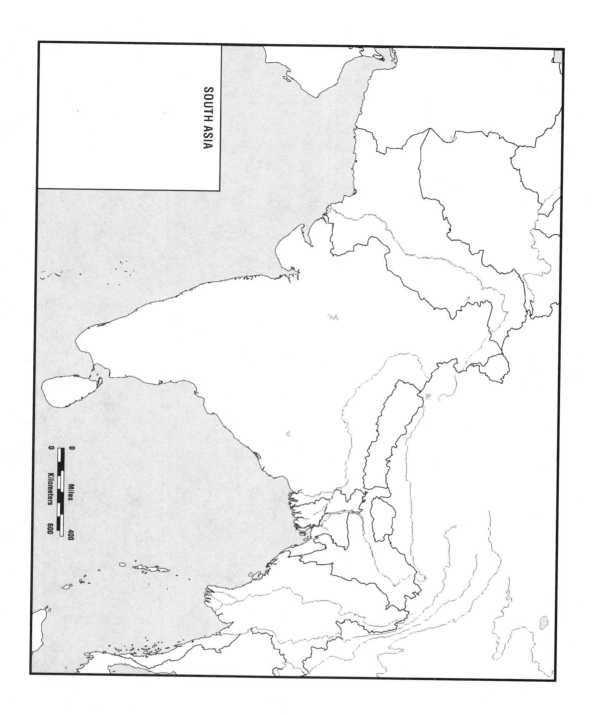

SOUTH ASIA

Miles

Kilometers

0
0
400
600

CHAPTER NINE
East Asia

LEARNING OBJECTIVES

After reading the chapter and working through this study guide, you should understand how the textbook's nine thematic concepts relate to East Asia.

- Climate change: Understand the different environmental problems East Asia is facing, including greenhouse gas emissions and global warming. Know the outcomes of these problems and how governments and citizens are trying to improve the situation.
- Democratization: Understand why this region has been democratizing. Also know how and why the Han Chinese majority dominates China, and what effects this has on the numerous ethnic groups in this region.
- Development: Know how ancient Chinese forms of government and philosophy have influenced the development of the economy, culture, politics, and gender roles. Understand how globalization has changed these, and how quality of life has been affected by recent development.
- Food: Know why more food needs to be imported to this region. Understand how food security and food production are related to urbanization and globalization.
- Gender: Know how gender attitudes are changing in the region. Understand family, work, and gender relationships in industrial areas of East Asia.
- Globalization: Know the differences between free market and Communist economic systems. Know what market reforms have been enacted in this region and their positive and negative consequences.
- Population: Know why population is still growing in this region even though growth rates are declining. Understand how population growth is putting strains on both human well-being and the environment. Know what is being done to attempt to control population growth.
- Urbanization: Understand the push and pull factors that result in rural-to-urban migration. Also know the effects that migrants, especially the floating population, have on cities.
- Water: Know how water affects agriculture as well as population distribution and density in the region. Also understand how some areas can experience water shortages, while other areas have a surfeit of water.

KEY TERMS

The following terms are in **bold** in the textbook. Page numbers for each term can be found in the Chapter Key Terms list at the end of the textbook chapter. In the space next to the term (or on a separate sheet or flash cards), you can fill in the definitions for reference or quiz yourself for exam review. Definitions are found in the glossary of the textbook, as well as in the sidebars on the page they first appear.

Ainu

alluvium (Subregions textbook version only)

Asia-Pacific region (Subregions textbook version only)

chaebol (Subregions textbook version only)

Confucianism

Cultural Revolution

export-led growth

floating population

food security

food self-sufficiency (Subregions textbook version only)

foreign investment

gers (or yurts) (Subregions textbook version only)

Great Leap Forward

growth poles

hukou system

kaizen system

kanban system

land reform

loess (Subregions textbook version only)

petty capitalists

qanats (Subregions textbook version only)

regional self-sufficiency

regional specialization

responsibility system

special economic zones (SEZs)

state-aided market economy

tsunami

typhoon

wet rice cultivation

yurts (or *gers*) (Subregions textbook version only)

REVIEW QUESTIONS
The following review questions are related directly to the textbook material. These questions can be used to help you prepare for an exam, or you may want to read through the questions before you begin reading the textbook, quizzing yourself after you complete each section.

The Geographic Setting
1. There are few flat surfaces in East Asia. Those that are flat are often either too cold or too dry for human use. What adaptations do East Asians make to be able to use this land?
2. Compare the climate, vegetation, and population of the dry interior and the monsoon east.
3. Why is climate change a growing concern in East Asia? How does its vulnerability to climate change relate to each of the following: water, urbanization, and flooding?
4. How is food security tied to globalization? Using both agriculture and fisheries as examples, make the argument that imported food is a sign of food security.
5. What are some of the problems with air quality in East Asia? How are these related to urbanization and population density?

6. What are some positive and negative effects that Confucianism had on political, economic, and social life?

7. Know some of the differences between the Kuomintang (KMT) and the Chinese Communist Party (CCP). Who backed them, who were their leaders, and what were their goals, philosophies, and impacts?

8. What factors contributed to Japan's transformation into a democratic nation and a giant in the global economy? How did the Japanese and the Chinese influence other countries in the region after World War II?

Current Geographic Issues

9. What are some of the differences between the economies of capitalist countries and Communist countries in the region? What are some of the positive and negative aspects of each?

10. How did Japan overcome isolation and destruction from World War II to become one of the world's wealthiest and most influential nations?

11. Did communal land reform work in China? Why or why not? What were the benefits and drawbacks of this system? How does the current land ownership/land use system of today relate to the communal system?

12. Why was China's policy of regional self-sufficiency encouraged? Discuss its successes. Have market reforms and globalization been more successful? Why or why not?

13. Why have urban areas grown, and why are there such disparities between rural and urban areas? What is life like in urban China?

14. What is some evidence that democratization is underway, and in some cases very well established, in the region? How has the international community sped up democratization?

15. What are some potential political, social, and economic changes that will come with an increase in information technology?

16. What are the potential financial and social costs of an aging population? How should the region respond to an aging population?

17. What effects will a growing population have on the economy, environment, and human well-being in China? What are some of the positive and negative effects China's one-child-per-family policy is having? Why does China's population continue to grow, even though couples are limited to one child?

18. Although there have been many improvements in quality of life, including health care, water quality, and literacy, what improvements are still necessary in this region?

19. How are minority groups treated in East Asia? Why are Han settlers being sent to regions that have large numbers of minorities? What are the effects of this resettlement?

20. What effects might China have on the rest of the world because of the migration of its people? What are the causes of this migration?

CRITICAL THINKING EXERCISES

The following questions ask you to apply the ideas and principles you learned from the textbook to new situations.

1. Confucian ideology and society

The Confucian ideology penetrated all aspects of Chinese society and deeply affected its social, economic, and political geography.

- A woman was confined to the domestic spaces of home and almost always placed under the authority of others: her parents, her husband, or her son. What might life have been like for women? What might life have been like for the men in the seat of authority?
- What might life have been like for the masses at the base of the hierarchical pyramid?
- Confucian values were used to organize the state and the economy, as well as society. Do you think people were better off with this ruling tradition? What would have been some other alternatives at the time?

2. The communal way of living

When the Communist party first came to power in China, it undertook land reform, which resulted in banding small landholders into cooperatives, then eventually into full-scale communes in an attempt to improve agricultural production.

- What were the benefits and drawbacks of the commune system? Do you think it did more good or more harm overall?
- Communes took over all aspects of life, including political organization, industry, health care, social life, and education. What would be some of the benefits and drawbacks in *your life* if you were forced to or chose to live communally?
- What would some obstacles be to instituting this type of system in the United States?

3. Would you invest in China?

China has begun to pursue a more efficient and market-oriented economy. It has become a participant in the global economy as a significant producer of manufactured goods, with a market of more than 1 billion customers.

- What factors would discourage you from investing or locating a business in China?
- What factors would encourage you to invest or locate a business in China?
- Based on the factors you've listed, would you invest or locate a business in China? What factor(s) really made the decision for you?
- Identify five changes that would have to take place in this region to make investing in China more attractive. Be sure to consider social, economic, political, and environmental factors.

4. The future of the extended family

In an attempt to reduce population growth in a country with already over one-fifth of the world's population, most Chinese couples are limited by law to one child. Within two generations, the kinship categories of sibling, cousin, aunt and uncle, and sister- and brother-in-law disappeared from families that complied with the policy.

- Because of the great value people put on an extended family in China, how do you think this will affect family life? How will it affect child and elder care? How will it affect social development or social conscience?

- How would this policy have affected *you* and *your family* if it were in place when your parents or grandparents were having children? What would it be like to have no siblings, cousins, or aunts and uncles?

- If you have siblings, consider who was first born in *your* set of siblings. Under a one-child policy, would you have been born? What might have happened in your family if the first born was a female? What if the first born was a male?

- How about when you have/had children? How would you feel about being legally limited to one child?

5. Tolerance of ethnic diversity in the Xinjiang Uygur Autonomous Region

Beijing's central authority has been under increasing challenge from Muslim separatists in Xinjiang Uygur in western China. The conflict has resulted in a significant loss of life and human rights violations against the Uygurs and violent incidents by separatists.

- Explore the following Web sites and identify examples of human rights violations in Xinjiang. Also, make a list of the four most commonly mentioned abuses.
    - www.amnestyusa.org – Amnesty International (search Uygur, Uyghur, or Uighur)
    - www.uyghuramerican.org – The Uyghur American Association
    - www.uyghurcongress.org – World Uyghur Congress

- There have also been a number of violent incidents that have been attributed to independence activists. Using these same Web sites, identify examples of violent incidents attributed to Muslim separatists.

- Thus far, the independence movement in Xinjiang Uygur has failed to generate widespread support and remains too fractured to present a meaningful threat to Beijing's rule. Why do you think this is the case?

- Do you think that the increasingly savage suppression of Muslim protests will generate unity and coordination within the various separatist groups in Xinjiang?

- What are the stakes in this conflict for both sides? Why are the Uygurs and the Beijing government in such conflict?

IMPORTANT PLACES

The following places are featured in the chapter. Make sure you can locate all of them on a map. Blank outline maps can be found on the textbook's Web site: www.whfreeman.com/pulsipher5e. Also, to prepare for quizzes and exams, write a few important facts about each place in the space provided.

Physical Features

1. Chang Jiang (Yangtze)

2. East China Sea

3. Gobi Desert

4. Gulf of Tonkin

5. Himalayas

6. Huang He (Yellow River)

7. Loess Plateau

8. Mekong River

9. Mount Fuji

10. Northeast China Plain

11. Ordos Desert

12. Pacific Ocean

13. Pacific Ring of Fire

14. Philippine Sea

15. Plateau of Tibet

16. Qaidam Basin

17. Sea of Japan

18. Sichuan Basin

19. South China Sea

20. Taklimakan Desert

21. Tarim Basin

22. Yellow Sea

23. Yunnan-Guizhou Plateau

24. Zhu Jiang (Pearl River)

Regions/Countries/States/Provinces
25. China

26. Guangdong

27. Japan

28. Macao

29. Mongolia

30. North Korea

31. South Korea

32. Taiwan

33. Tibet (Xizang)

34. Xinjiang Uygur

Cities/Urban Areas
35. Beijing

36. Hong Kong

37. Kyoto

38. P'yongyang

39. Seoul

40. Shanghai

41. Taipei

42. Tokyo

43. Ulan Bator

MAPPING EXERCISES

The following mapping exercises are designed to improve your knowledge of the location of places, underscore why they are important, and clarify how they relate to one another. Some questions will ask you to locate places, compare maps, or fill in data; others will test your understanding of *why* you were asked to map the features that you did. Use the blank outline maps at the end of the chapter to complete these exercises. Additional blank outline maps can be found on the textbook's Web site: www.whfreeman.com/pulsipher5e.

1. Population, landforms, and human modifications and adaptations

Of the few flat surfaces in the rugged landscapes of East Asia, many are too cold or too dry to be useful to humans.

- On a blank map of East Asia, shade the areas (in red) that have over 1300 persons per square mile (over 500 people per square kilometer) (Photo Essay 9.6).
- From Figure 9.1 (regional map), shade (in tan) and label the location of the Gobi, Ordos, and Taklimakan deserts.
- Trace with a thick blue line and label the following rivers: Chang Jiang (Yangtze), Huang He (Yellow River), Mekong River, Nu (Salween), and Zhu Jiang (Pearl River). Mark the location of the Three Gorges Dam.
- Draw (with ^^^) and label the location of the Himalayas.
- Draw a hatch pattern over and label the Plateau of Tibet and Yunnan-Guizhou Plateau.

Questions

    a. Is population concentrated near any particular type of landform(s)?

    b. Which type of landform is associated with low/no population concentrations?

    c. In cases where population is not located near a water source, how might people adapt to make agriculture productive? Discuss the benefits of the Three Gorges Dam.

    d. In cases where population is located near rugged terrain, what adaptations might people make to create space for agriculture?

    e. In light of East Asia's vulnerability to climate change (Photo Essay 9.2) how might the map of population density change in the future? Explain your response.

2. Economic growth, SEZs, and ETDZs

Special economic zones (SEZs) and economic and technology development zones (ETDZs) are central to China's new market reforms and have rapidly opened the economy to international trade.

- Using Figure 9.16 (map of foreign investment), on the blank map of China and its provinces, draw a blue square for each SEZ and a red dot for each ETDZ.
- Using Figure 9.15 (map of rural-urban GDP per capita disparities), shade the provinces in yellow that have $3001-5000 GDP per capita, and shade the provinces in orange that have $5001-$10,444 GDP per capita.

Questions

a. What type of general relationship did you expect to find between the SEZs/ETDZs and GDP per capita? Explain why SEZs/ETDZs might affect GDP per capita.

b. Are there provinces with SEZs/ETDZs that don't have an upper-middle or high GDP? Provide at least two reasons why do you think this is the case.

c. Assume that SEZs/ETDZs are major growth poles (drawing more investment and migration) and examine the map of population density (Photo Essay 9.6), the map of migration (Figure 9.2), and Photo Essay 9.4 on urbanization in East Asia.

   - What will happen to those provinces with SEZs/ETDZs that already have high population densities (consider the environment, infrastructure, and resulting living conditions)?

   - Why do you think the government has chosen to put SEZs/ETDZs in areas with low population densities? What effects might SEZs/ETDZs have on these areas? What effect will these have on rural-urban disparities?

3. Three Gorges Dam

Although the Three Gorges Dam is expected to save millions of lives and much property, the 370-mile long reservoir it created has drowned 62,000 acres of farmland, 13 major cities, 140 large towns, hundreds of small villages, and 1600 factories, displacing over 1.9 million people.

- On the blank map of the Central China subregion, draw the Chang Jiang with a thick blue line.
- Using the map of population density (Photo Essay 9.6), shade in areas that have more than 1300 people per square mile (over 500 people per square kilometer).
- Using the map of foreign investment (Figure 9.16), draw a red circle for each ETDZ and a blue square for each SEZ.
- Using the maps on the University of Hong Kong's Civil Engineering Computer Aided Learning (CIVCAL) Web site (civcal.media.hku.hk/threegorges/Default.htm), draw in the location of the dam.
- Also, using the maps on the CIVCAL Web site, draw the outline, showing the extent of the reservoir created by the Three Gorges Dam.

a. Based on the outline of the reservoir, what cities or urban areas are affected and how?
b. Will this dam negatively affect any of the ETDZs or SEZs by flooding them or reducing the amount of water flowing in the area? Which ones?
c. Will the dam/reservoir bring any ETDZs or SEZs *more* business? Which ones and why?
d. Using the University of Hong Kong's Web site and your textbook, identify two positive effects the dam/reservoir might have on each of the following: society, politics, and the environment. Identify at two negative effects the dam/reservoir might have on each of the following: society, politics, and the environment.

SAMPLE EXAM QUESTIONS

The following are sample questions to help you review for an exam. Answers are found in the back of this study guide.

1. Which statement is not true of the majority of internal migrants within China?
a) They are illegal migrants without residency rights.
b) They are dependent on their employers for housing.
c) They are offered a specific career track that helps them get promoted and earn more money within two years of taking a factory job.
d) They use most of the money they earn to buy food and send back home to their families.

2. Which of the following is not an explanation for the shrinking of fertile zones in East Asia?
a) longer monsoon seasons
b) urban development
c) industrial expansion
d) agricultural mismanagement

3. Which of the following is not a serious criticism of China's Three Gorges Dam?
a) The hydroelectric power generated by the dam will not be significant.
b) The dam is constructed over a seismic fault.
c) The giant sturgeon's spawning grounds have been lost and the fish may become extinct.
d) Cracks in the dam raise doubts regarding its structural integrity.

4. Which of the following accurately reflects the issue of water in China in recent years?
a) The government encourages debate in the media about the problem of water pollution.
b) The flood hazard has been eliminated by an extensive flood control system.
c) Water problems, including flooding and drought, have increased substantially due to intense human alteration of the landscape.
d) Water quality in cities has increased dramatically due to the use of solar water purifiers.

5. Which of the following was not a result of the Cultural Revolution?
a) People were not permitted to be part of any type of organized religion.
b) Petty traders were punished for being capitalists.
c) Agriculture was eliminated and farmers were forced to work in factories.
d) Scientists and scholars were sent to work in the mines and industries.

6. Which of the following is the most accurate characterization of the Japanese model of government-guided free market economy that served Japan so successfully in the decades following World War II?
a) A small, flexible bureaucracy provides enforcement of regulations and collects taxes, leaving the free market to operate without interference.
b) A powerful bureaucracy determines production levels and resource commitments to domestic industries, which are all state-owned.
c) A strong bureaucracy provides financial assistance, advice, and protection from foreign competition to domestic industrial enterprises.
d) A small bureaucracy maintains a high level of economic efficiency by ensuring multiple domestic and foreign competitors.

7. Which of the following is not one of the problems associated with the growth of rural enterprises in modern China?
a) They contribute to women's lack of status and their role as second-class citizens.
b) They have been linked to corruption and organized crime.
c) They tend to cluster around coastal cities, rather than creating jobs in the hinterland.
d) They pollute waterways and add to air pollution.

8. Which statement best summarizes urban-rural disparities in East Asia?
a) Urban areas have better access to jobs, health care, and education than rural areas.
b) Urban areas have better air quality than rural areas.
c) Rural areas have much higher crime rates than urban areas.
d) Rural areas have much greater population density than rural areas.

9. Which of the following is not an explanation for the low rate of natural increase in China?
a) the one-child-per-family policy
b) urbanization
c) changing gender roles
d) Confucianism

10. The first international agreement to reduce greenhouse gas emissions was signed in the East Asian city of:
a) Tokyo.
b) Beijing.
c) Ulan Bator.
d) Kyoto.

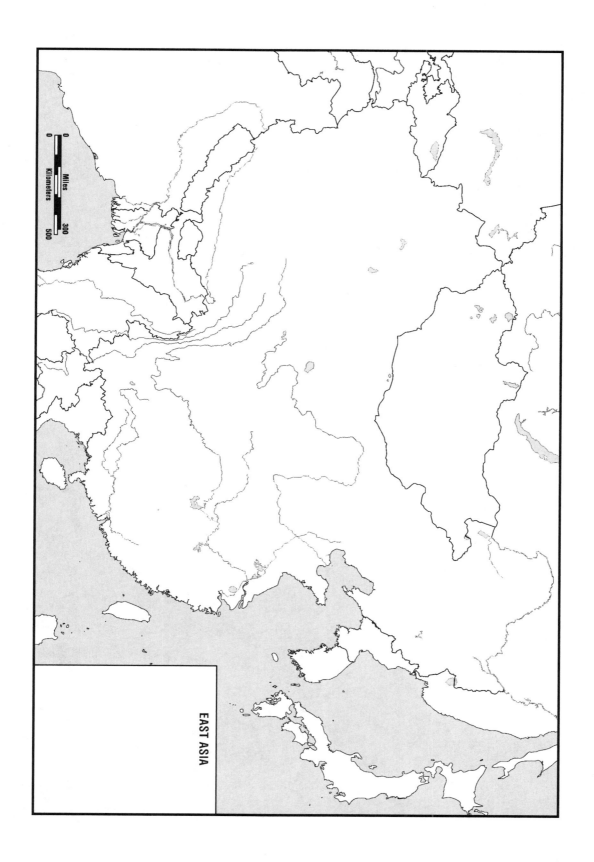

EAST ASIA

East Asia

171

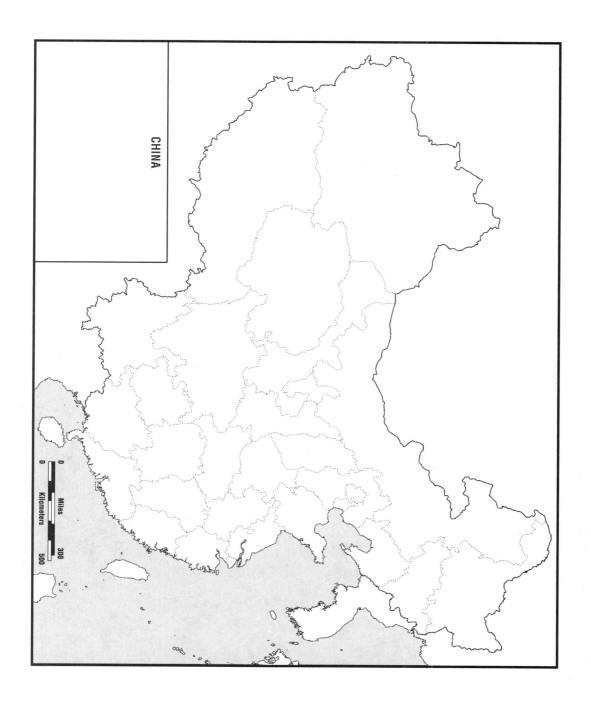

CHINA

0 | Miles | 300
0 | Kilometers | 500

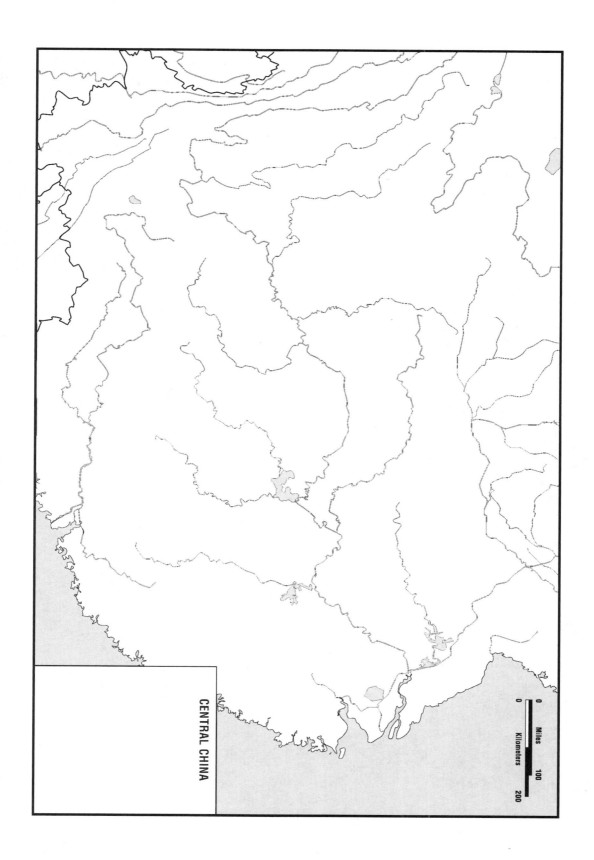

CENTRAL CHINA

CHAPTER TEN
Southeast Asia

LEARNING OBJECTIVES

After reading the chapter and working through this study guide, you should understand how the textbook's nine thematic concepts relate to Southeast Asia.

- Climate change: Know the relationship between wide-scale burning of the tropical forest and global climate change. Be able to identify specific regional effects resulting from climate change.
- Democratization: Know which countries have transitioned to democratic governance and know which have not. At the same time understand the challenges that countries face when transitioning to democracy.
- Development: Be able to identify the pros and cons of regional and global trade activities in the context of worker rights and environmental impacts.
- Food: Know the carrying capacity of the land and relate it to the region's current population. Understand the impact of food production on the tropical forests.
- Gender: Be able to identify the long-standing cultural reasons that help to explain the relatively high status of women in this region.
- Globalization: Understand how many of the countries in this region have used their physical location to create strong linkages with the global economy. Be able to identify the push and pull factors related to the international migration of workers.
- Population: Understand the general improvements in living standards but be able to identify pockets of habitation where poverty remains. Know the reasons that have motivated indigenous people to become more outspoken regarding their land rights and cultural practices.
- Urbanization: Understand the phenomenon of the primate city in the context of Southeast Asian countries. Be able to identify the most pressing problems faced by cities in this region.
- Water: Understand the role of the intertropical convergence zone in producing rain in the region. Be able to explain El Niño's impacts on the region's climate. Understand how the source region of rivers can affect downstream flow.

KEY TERMS

The following terms are in **bold** in the textbook. Page numbers for each term can be found in the Chapter Key Terms list at the end of the textbook chapter. In the space next to the term (or on a separate sheet or flash cards), you can fill in the definitions for reference or quiz yourself for exam review. Definitions are found in the glossary of the textbook, as well as in the sidebars on the page they first appear.

archipelago

Association of Southeast Asian Nations (ASEAN)

Australo-Melanesians

Austronesians

coral bleaching

crony capitalism

cultural pluralism

detritus

doi moi (Subregions textbook version only)

domino theory

El Niño

feminization of labor

foreign exchange

resettlement schemes

sex tourism

REVIEW QUESTIONS

The following review questions are related directly to the textbook material. These questions can be used to help you prepare for an exam, or you may want to read through the questions before you begin reading the textbook, quizzing yourself after you complete each section.

The Current Geographic Setting

1. Explain how plate tectonics play a role in creating the conditions for active volcanism and earthquakes in the Philippines and Indonesia. What is the impact of these natural processes on human life in this region?

2. Explain how the monsoons and ITCZ bring rain to Southeast Asia most of the year, and discuss the ways in which El Niño and La Niña interrupt or exaggerate rainfall.

3. Name at least three practices that account for the greatest depletion of the tropical forests. Does this surprise you? Why or why not? Deforestation leads to what other general environmental problems?

4. How does food production in this region contribute to climate change? Of the three agricultural systems described in the textbook, which appears to have the largest impact on climate change? Why? How do increasing population densities correlate with food production to exaggerate impacts of global climate change?

5. The human settlement of Southeast Asia is ancient. Describe the two prehistoric waves of people into the region and the landforms that facilitated this settlement. Where have settlers come from in the last 2000 years? What has prompted these newer waves of migration?

6. Describe the conditions under which Europe, the United States, and Japan colonized various parts of Southeast Asia at different times. When was independence achieved in the various colonies and under what conditions?

Current Geographic Issues

7. How did national governments use import substitution industries and Export Processing Zones (EPZs) as successful economic development strategies?

8. How is crony capitalism a unique form of corruption?

9. What factors led to the economic crisis of the late 1990s? What procedures or practices helped the countries pull out of the crisis?

10. What role is ASEAN playing to help the region's economic development? How do policies/practices of ASEAN resemble trade bloc practices elsewhere in the world?

11. What factors have led to increasing democratization in Indonesia? What are some indications that these factors would be appropriate in other Southeast Asian countries that are verging on full democratization?

12. What indicators suggest that this region is nearing the last stage of the demographic transition model?

13. Where has population grown most rapidly? Why? Where are densities high? Why? Where is population relatively sparse? Why? How is population change correlated with wealth and poverty in the region?

14. How do religious and cultural traditions promote the transmission of HIV-AIDS?
15. What is the role of sex tourism in development? Why is this detrimental to overall development?
16. How does rural-to-urban migration affect agriculture? How can countries solve these problems? List three push factors and three pull factors of migration. How do resettlement schemes solve some problems while exacerbating others?
17. What major religions are important in the region? To some extent, different religions are associated with different ethnic groups and parts of the region. Describe the alignments for Animism (traditional), Buddhism, Islam, Hinduism, and Christianity.
18. Why are the Overseas (ethnic) Chinese criticized in the region?
19. What has been the impact of modernization on family structures? What are the benefits of these changes? What are the challenges?
20. Women play important and powerful roles in Southeast Asia. Discuss at least three aspects of society and family life that illustrate this fact.

CRITICAL THINKING EXERCISES

The following questions ask you to apply the ideas and principles you learned from the textbook to new situations.

1. Burma and Thailand: How can two neighbors be so different?

Burma and Thailand share a common border and part of the Malay Peninsula, yet their historical paths and current status are vastly different.

* Compare and contrast the historical and current political, social, and economic characteristics of these two neighbors.
* What expectations do you have for each country's development during the twenty-first century? Justify your expectations.
* Will these two neighbors ever share common development goals? Defend your response.

2. Vietnam: Two generations' perspectives

Many people born during the last 25 years of the twentieth century have little or no memory of the Vietnam conflict.

* Develop three questions that are of interest to you and interview someone you know who served in Vietnam during the Vietnam War. You may want to do some research on the Vietnam War first.
* Ideally, see if you can find Vietnamese people who have now immigrated to the United States and remember the Vietnam conflict. Ask them the same questions.
* Interview two of your fellow students and ask them the same questions. If possible, find Vietnamese or Vietnamese-American students on campus and interview them.
* Draw some conclusions about different generations' and different nationalities' attitudes about Vietnam and about the conflict.

3. ASEAN's growing membership

ASEAN seeks to form a regional trade membership by using the North American Free Trade Agreement (NAFTA) and the European Union (EU) as models.

- What are positive and negative aspects of membership in ASEAN for the current members? Think about each country's economic situation and what it has to gain or lose as a member of ASEAN.
- Why does ASEAN want to bring in the poorer countries of Southeast Asia? How can current ASEAN members benefit by bringing in these poorer members? How can the poorer countries benefit?
- Make a prediction about the future of the ASEAN countries with regards to economic growth and human well-being. Be sure you justify your prediction based on your earlier arguments.

4. Coping with fragmentation

Several Southeast Asian countries are fragmented spatially. For instance, Indonesia is spread across an archipelago that includes 17,000 islands.

- What challenges do the governments of these fragmented countries face in trying to establish a strong centralized power?
- What economic, political, and social challenges arise from this fragmentation?
- How do people whose geographical separation, which is often associated with weak nationalistic ties, develop a sense of commitment to one national government?
- Identify case studies from the textbook or current news articles that emphasize the impact of spatial fragmentation on the development of a nationalistic spirit.

5. Mechanization of agriculture, labor issues, and economic development

The textbook mentions the increasing role of mechanization in agriculture and even one of the photographs shows large machinery in use on rice paddies.

- What does mechanization of agriculture tell us about the role of small family farms and large corporate farms? What does it tell us about the government's attitude toward corporate farming?
- What does mechanization of agriculture have to do with the continued movement of people away from rural areas and into the urban settings?
- What is the relationship between mechanized agriculture and the disappearance of the region's tropical forests?
- After considering each of these questions, come to a conclusion about the benefits or challenges of mechanized farming in this region, then make some recommendations accordingly.
- Select one of the following key players and evaluate how your decision matches or conflicts with the impact of mechanized farming on their lives: a small plot farmer and his family, a young married couple, both of whom have high school educations and choose to move from their farm village into a larger town, an elderly couple who has farmed by hand labor all of their lives and are now thinking of selling their small farm to a neighbor who is wealthy enough to mechanize his farming, the elderly couple's neighbor.

IMPORTANT PLACES

The following places are featured in the chapter. Make sure you can locate all of them on a map. Blank outline maps can be found on the textbook's Web site: www.whfreeman.com/pulsipher5e. Also, to prepare for quizzes and exams, write a few important facts about each place in the space provided.

Physical Features

1. Andaman Sea

2. Bali

3. Black River

4. Borneo

5. Chao Phraya River

6. Greater Mekong Basin

7. Gulf of Thailand

8. Indian Ocean

9. Irrawaddy River

10. Java

11. Langkawi

12. Lesser Sunda Islands

13. Lombok

14. Luzon

15. Malay Peninsula

16. Mekong River and Delta

17. Mindanao

18. Molucca Islands

19. New Guinea

20. Pacific Ring of Fire

21. Red River

22. Salween River

23. South China Sea

24. Strait of Malacca

25. Sulawesi (Celebes Islands)

26. Sumatra

27. Timor Island

28. Tonle Sap Lake

29. Tubbataha Reef

Regions/Countries/States/Provinces
30. Aceh

31. Brunei

32. Burma (Myanmar)

33. Cambodia

34. East Timor (Timor-Leste)

35. French Indochina

36. Indonesia

37. Kalimantan

38. Laos

39. Malaysia

40. Philippines

41. Sarawak

42. Shan

43. Singapore

44. Thailand

45. Vietnam

46. West Papua

Cities/Urban Areas

47. Banda Aceh

48. Bandung

49. Bangkok

50. Chau Doc

51. Chiang Mai

52. Davao

53. Dien Bien Phu

54. Dili

55. Hanoi

56. Ho Chi Minh City (Saigon)

57. Jakarta

58. Kuala Lumpur

59. Luang Prabang

60. Lucban

61. Manila

62. Penan

63. Phnom Penh

64. Rangoon

65. Tegal

66. Udon Thani

67. Vientiane

MAPPING EXERCISES

The following mapping exercises are designed to improve your knowledge of the location of places, underscore why they are important, and clarify how they relate to one another. Some questions will ask you to locate places, compare maps, or fill in data; others will test your understanding of *why* you were asked to map the features that you did. Use the blank outline maps at the end of the chapter to complete these exercises. Additional blank outline maps can be found on the textbook's Web site: www.whfreeman.com/pulsipher5e.

1. Tourism and indigenous peoples

Tourism is suggested as a good alternative for regional and local economic development in Southeast Asia. However, indigenous peoples may be adversely affected while they, at the same time, reap economic benefits.

- Using Figure 10.3 (map of indigenous groups), and especially the inset map, shade the indigenous groups' locations on a blank map of Southeast Asia.
- Draw in the approximate location of the Asian highway system, using Figure 10.16 (map of transportation infrastructure).
- Finally, use Photo Essay 10.5 to cross hatch (///) areas with population densities of 651 or more people per square mile (251 or more people per square kilometer).

Questions

    a. Based on your map, as well as the reading of the beginning essay on community-based mapping projects, and location of such tourist locations as Angkor Wat, the Mekong Delta, Tubbataha Reef, and the northern Sumatran coast, identify areas where indigenous peoples will be highly affected by the tourist industry.

    b. Suggest benefits to the indigenous peoples in the places you have identified. Make a judgment as to the sustainability of those benefits.

    c. Suggest special challenges these indigenous people may face and discuss how their culture can be protected.

    d. Propose policies and practices that will protect indigenous cultures and livelihoods while still bringing economic opportunities to indigenous groups.

2. Agriculture and population density

Population density can often be related to economic lifestyles; even varying types of agricultural systems are often associated with different population densities.

- On a blank map of Southeast Asia, label all of the countries in the region.
- Using Figure 10.9 (map of agricultural patterns), shade intensive cropland.
- Using Photo Essay 10.5 (map of population density), cross hatch (///) the areas with 651 or more people per square mile (251 or more people per square kilometer).

<u>Questions</u>

    a. What is the relationship between intensity of agricultural pursuits and population density?

    b. Are there any anomalies? If so, where are they? Explain them.

    c. Based on your reading of the descriptions of food production in the textbook, along with careful examination of photographs throughout the chapter, estimate the type of farming system used in the most densely populated areas and in the most sparsely populated areas. Justify your decision.

3. The Diaspora of Southeast Asian women

Over 50 percent of the people who engage in extraregional migration are women. Many of these women move within the region as well as to other world regions to find work as maids.

- Using Table 10.3 (gender comparisons), draw a graduated circle in each country to represent women's earned income as a percent of men's. Remember to make the smallest circle correspond to the lowest range of female earned income as a percent of male earned income.
- Again, using Table 10.3, select gray shades to shade female enrollment in education for all countries. Remember to use the lightest gray for the lowest levels of enrollment and the darkest shade for the highest level of enrollment.

<u>Questions</u>

    a. Refer to the "maid trade" map (Figure 10.20) and identify three countries in this region that appear to be major contributors to the "maid trade." Explain any relationships you see between percent of female income and female education enrollment and countries' contribution to the "maid trade."

    b. If no relationship is suggested by the map, then using your understanding of this region, suggest other reasons for a country's high "maid trade" numbers.

SAMPLE EXAM QUESTIONS

The following are sample questions to help you review for an exam. Answers are found in the back of this study guide.

1. Which island is home to three countries: Indonesia, Malaysia, and Brunei?
a) Hokkaido
b) Borneo
c) Sumatra
d) Java

2. Tectonic forces in Southeast Asia are responsible for all of the following except:
a) earthquakes.
b) tsunamis.
c) monsoons.
d) mudslides.

3. Which of the following theories could best explain the presence of ancient humans and Asian land animals on the islands of Southeast Asia?
a) They crossed from the mainland along temporarily exposed pieces of land that are now submerged in the ocean.
b) They reached and were spread throughout the islands by seaborne traders as they went from one island to the next.
c) During periodic ice ages, glaciers extended from the coastline of the mainland to many of the islands.
d) Until an earthquake destroyed it, Huxley's Line provided a narrow land connection to the islands.

4. The result of El Niño in Southeast Asia is usually:
a) earthquakes.
b) volcanic eruptions.
c) drought.
d) flooding.

5. All of the following are the effects of deforestation in Southeast Asia except:
a) loss of habitat for native animal species.
b) higher rates of malaria and schistosomiasis.
c) emissions of greenhouse gases.
d) loss of living space for indigenous peoples.

6. Which statement best summarizes the environmental impact of oil palm plantations in Southeast Asia?
a) Their activities are carbon-neutral, making them an excellent source of economic development.
b) The fires created to clear the land for oil palm plantations can smolder underground for years, releasing huge amounts of toxic emissions into the atmosphere.
c) Because palms are grown primarily with green agricultural techniques, the impact of plantations on the atmosphere is negligible.
d) The oil palm plantations of Southeast Asia are the world's largest contributor to global climate change.

7. According to the textbook, how did Thailand manage to maintain its independence during the European colonial era?
a) It used diplomatic acumen to acquire protective services of the Soviet Union
b) It poured resources into its military technologies that rivaled those of Europe
c) It undertook a large-scale push to modernize itself in the European mold
d) It assertively established its own colonies to serve as buffers around its territory

8. Which of the following is the most appropriate description of crony capitalism in Southeast Asia?
a) Personal and familial connections among politicians, bankers, and entrepreneurs are used to create economic opportunities.
b) Close ties formed among small groups of states allow them to jointly coordinate development projects.
c) Private interests make investment decisions while state planners have responsibility for daily business operations.
d) Companies invest outside of their areas of specialization in order to control all stages of the production process.

9. Which of the following is not an explanation for increased rates of HIV-AIDS infection in Southeast Asia?
a) Religious organizations restrict public sex education.
b) Sex workers and truck drivers have high rates of infection and transmit the disease over a wide geographic area.
c) Local customs support sexual experimentation for men.
d) Government organizations never offer programs to support condom use.

10. Which of the following is not true of the "maid trade" in Southeast Asia?
a) Most of the maids are uneducated women who work as maids to support their families.
b) The maid trade increased exponentially after the economic crisis of the 1990s.
c) Most Indonesian maids work in the Persian Gulf.
d) The Philippine government requires Filipinas working abroad to be given Sundays off.

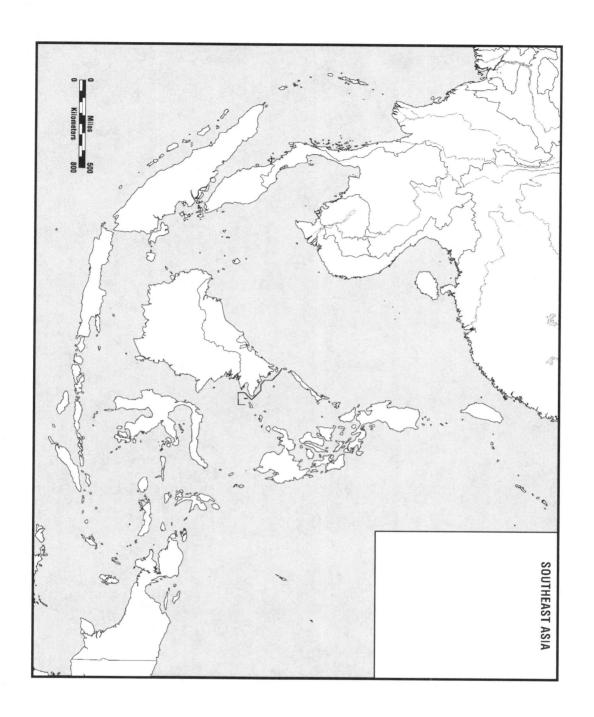

SOUTHEAST ASIA

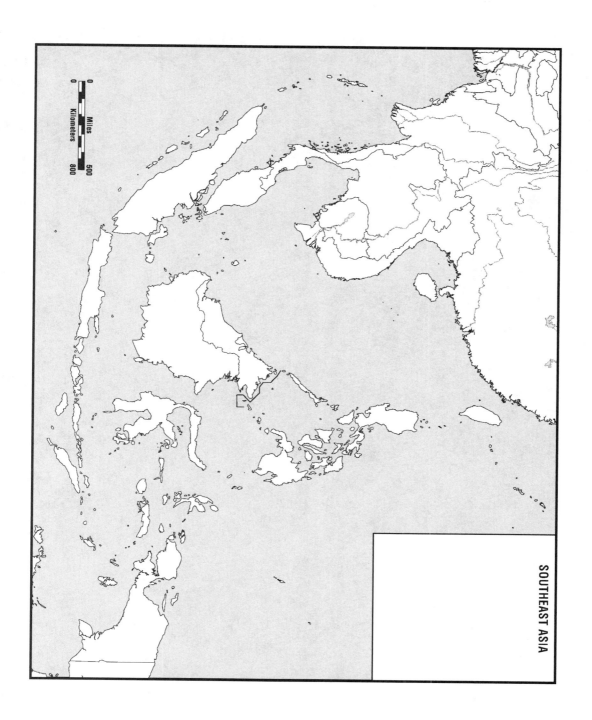

SOUTHEAST ASIA

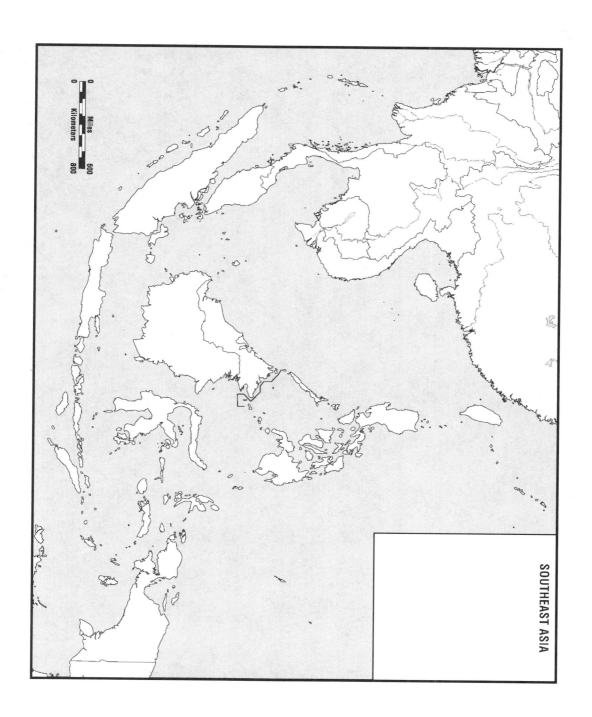

SOUTHEAST ASIA

CHAPTER ELEVEN
Oceania: Australia, New Zealand, and the Pacific

LEARNING OBJECTIVES

After reading the chapter and working through this study guide, you should understand how the textbook's nine thematic concepts relate to Oceania.

- Climate change: While the contribution of this region to global climate change is small, the region is overly burdened with effects of such dramatic change. Understand why sea level rise is the major environmental factor with which the entire region must cope.

- Democratization: A few of the islands are still part of a diminished colonial empire belonging to European states and the United States. Democratic systems dominate, but when crises arise, understand why some residents of the region suggest that the Pacific Way may be a more democratic and egalitarian way to manage local and national affairs.

- Development: Be able to explain why GDP per capita does not always tell the full story for this region and use the concept of subsistence affluence and the practice of MIRAB in your explanation.

- Food: Know why the region is fully capable of producing adequate food, and why New Zealand and Australia are large exporters of food products to primarily Asian states.

- Gender: Be able to explain how gender roles in the area are changing. Know how the rugged individualism associated with Australian men has changed, and how women throughout the region exert influence in the public domain.

- Globalization: Know the reasons for the shift in the relationship between this region and the rest of the world. Know why the historical relationship with the United States and Europe has been traded for ties with Asia and what economic organization helps support these new ties.

- Population: Know the historic bases for the diffusion of cultures across great expanses of ocean. Be able to identify the root causes for population growth in the region.

- Urbanization: Understand the urbanization rates in the countries of this region, where the urban concentrations are located, and how this concentration is problematical in the context of global climate change.

- Water: While water is a major factor in any discussion of this region, ample water is not always guaranteed. Be able to identify concerns based on access to and availability of fresh water supplies.

KEY TERMS

The following terms are in **bold** in the textbook. Page numbers for each term can be found in the Chapter Key Terms list at the end of the textbook chapter. In the space next to the term (or on a separate sheet or flash cards), you can fill in the definitions for reference or quiz yourself for exam review. Definitions are found in the glossary of the textbook, as well as in the sidebars on the page they first appear.

Aborigines

atoll

endemic

Gondwana

Great Barrier Reef

high islands

hot spots

invasive species

Maori

marsupials

Melanesia

Melanesians

Micronesia

MIRAB economy

monotremes

noble savage

Pacific Way

pidgin

Polynesia

roaring forties

subsistence affluence

REVIEW QUESTIONS

The following review questions are related directly to the textbook material. These questions can be used to help you prepare for an exam, or you may want to read through the questions before you begin reading the textbook, quizzing yourself after you complete each section.

The Geographic Setting

1. How are indigenous cultural traditions being revived to celebrate or portray a multicultural image of the region?

2. Compare the geologic forces that account for the location and features of this region. What are the differences between these geological forces that create low atolls vis-à-vis those that create high islands? How are *makatea* formed?

3. Compare the climate and moisture patterns of Australia and New Zealand. How does climate affect agricultural production in these two countries?

4. What is the impact of the El Niño weather phenomenon on the islands in the Pacific?

5. Why are so many species of plants and animals endemic to certain places in Oceania? What is wrong with thinking that simply importing a natural predator of an exotic species can cure the ill effects of introducing that exotic species in the first place?

6. What human actions and global environmental crises have had a profound impact on the region's environmental status? How are the region's people responding?

7. How does the region's role as a producer of raw materials impact its environment? Name two countries that have been victims of massive resource removal and describe why the impact is so disastrous.

8. What are the impacts (both positive and negative) of the United Nations Convention on the Law of the Sea on this region?

9. Why are islands in Micronesia, Melanesia, and Polynesia classified into these three major groups? What role did historical migrations play in these classifications?

10. What types of Europeans first colonized Australia and New Zealand, and how did the origins of European settlers shift over time?

11. Define the term "Asianization." Describe how attitudes toward Asianization have changed in the last fifty years. Explain what has brought about such change.

12. Describe the two population patterns in the region, and account for the differences.

13. Where is Australia's population concentrated? What accounts for this pattern? List at least three key challenges faced by urbanizing areas and explain the root causes of these challenges.

14. Why should Oceania be included in the international economic organization known as APEC? What does Oceania have to gain from participation and membership?

15. How did markets for Australia's and New Zealand's products change during the last half of the twentieth century? What accounts for the shift toward Asia? What were the economic impacts of these changes on Australia and New Zealand?

16. List challenges and opportunities that tourism brings to this region. How are countries adapting to the challenges?

17. What factors contribute to the new respect being shown for indigenous peoples of the region? What lessons can be learned from the indigenous perspective of land ownership that might help with environmental protection throughout the world?

18. The Pacific Way seems to have started from a concern about using colonial-dominated school curricula. What does it encompass today? What other practices are serving as unifying measures for this far flung region? How do they relate to the ideals of the Pacific Way?

19. New ways of life for women and men are emerging in this region. Discuss the varied historical roles of gender in Oceania and how modern life is affecting what men and women do and the ways they interact.

20. Compare and contrast the economic principle of subsistence affluence with the economic practice of MIRAB. How does each insulate Pacific island economies from some of the advantages and disadvantages of global market economies?

CRITICAL THINKING EXERCISES

The following questions ask you to apply the ideas and principles you learned from the textbook to new situations.

1. Australia's immigration policies: Changes over time

Australia's immigrant population, if identified by century of migration to Australia, reflects distinct changes in the country's immigration policies.

- Draw a time line that is divided into the 1700s, 1800s, 1900s, and the beginning years of the twenty-first century.

- Indicate the years of the changes in Australia's immigration policies as specific points on your time line.

- Underneath the time line, indicate the top three source countries for immigration during each century.

- Evaluate the impact of immigration reform on Australia's population as a whole and identify impacts on various labor groups (e.g., professionals, blue-collar workers, and Aborigines) within Australian society.

2. Mobility in a far-flung region

Even though islands of this region are small pieces of land dispersed over a large body of water, the people have always managed to move about, share material culture, and communicate.

- Identify forms of mobility that the book describes for inhabitants of the islands in the twenty-first century.
- Make some comparisons between your personal mobility patterns and the mobility patterns of the people who live on islands. What is different? What is the same?
- Finally, think in terms of impact. How does your personal mobility have an impact on your community or society? How does this compare with the impact that personal mobility in the islands has on their community or society?

3. A new syncretic cultural tradition

The attitudes toward, and roles of, indigenous peoples are changing in this region. Indigenous ways are now blending with practices introduced by European colonization.

- Write one sentence that argues in favor of the syncretic (blending) of cultural traditions that you read about in the textbook. The Haka Tradition is a good example.
- Now, reflect on your own community and identify at least two possible cultural syncretic processes that you see taking place around you. Can you still argue in favor of syncretic blending? Why or why not?

4. Internet technology in a region of great distances

Some suggest that Internet technology may provide a valuable opportunity for this region to become more closely interconnected.

- Make a list of at least three ways that Internet technology could serve as a vector for communication and connection for this region. Check the CIA World Factbook for information on individual countries' Internet technology access/use: www.cia.gov/cia/publications/factbook.
- Beside each suggested use of the Internet, identify positive and negative impacts of the application of Internet technology.
- Compare how your suggestions of technology for Oceania are similar or dissimilar to applications in your own community and life.

5. Living in the twenty-first century in a remote island nation

Place yourself as a citizen on one of the island nations discussed in this chapter. Imagine that you are a university student hoping to acquire adequate education to pursue a professional career.

- Based on your understanding of Oceania, suggest some of the cultural characteristics that would be particular to you if you had grown up in a traditional island culture.

- Based on this same understanding of Oceania, suggest challenges that you would face in acquiring this education, searching for a related employment opportunity, and how such activities would affect your connection to your homeland.
- Suggest the adaptations that you would have to make as you complete your education and move into your professional career. Consider issues related to gender, a rural or semi-rural background, and indigenous cultural roots.

IMPORTANT PLACES

The following places are featured in the chapter. Make sure you can locate all of them on a map. Blank outline maps can be found on the textbook's Web site: www.whfreeman.com/pulsipher5e. Also, to prepare for quizzes and exams, write a few important facts about each place in the space provided.

Physical Features

1. Uluru (Ayers Rock)

2. Bikini atoll

3. Blue Mountains

4. Bora-Bora

5. Caroline Islands

6. Cook Islands

7. Coral Sea

8. Darling River

9. Easter Island

10. Eastern Highlands (Great Dividing Range)

11. Galápagos Islands

12. Great Australian Bight

13. Great Barrier Reef

14. Gulf of Carpentaria

15. Indian Ocean

16. Kosrae

17. Milford Sound

18. Murray River

19. New Guinea

20. Northern Mariana Islands

21. Pacific Ocean

22. Reao Island

23. Ring of Fire

24. Samoa Islands

25. Satawal Island

26. Southern Alps

27. South Pacific Ocean

28. Tahiti

29. Tasman Sea

30. Tasmania

31. Yap

Regions/Countries/States/Provinces
32. Australia

33. Federated States of Micronesia

34. French Polynesia

35. Guam

36. Hawaii

37. Kiribati

38. Marshall Islands

39. Melanesia

40. Micronesia

41. Nauru

42. New Caledonia

43. New Zealand

44. Palau

45. Papua New Guinea

46. Polynesia

47. Republic of the Fiji Islands

48. Queensland

49. Samoa

50. Solomon Islands

51. South Australia

52. Tonga

53. Tuvalu

54. Vanuatu

55. Victoria

Cities/Urban Areas

56. Alice Springs

57. Apia

58. Auckland

59. Bougainville

60. Brisbane

61. Canberra

62. Christchurch

63. Funafuti

64. Honiara

65. Honolulu

66. Jandowae

67. Koror

68. Lyttleton

69. Majuro

70. Marlborough

71. Melbourne

72. Newcastle

73. Newton

74. Nuku'alofa

75. Palikir

76. Papeete

77. Perth

78. Port Moresby

79. Port-Vila

80. Suva

81. Sydney

82. Tarawa

83. Wellington

84. White Cliffs

85. Yalata

86. Yaren

MAPPING EXERCISES

The following mapping exercises are designed to improve your knowledge of the location of places, underscore why they are important, and clarify how they relate to one another. Some questions will ask you to locate places, compare maps, or fill in data; others will test your understanding of *why* you were asked to map the features that you did. Use the blank outline maps at the end of the chapter to complete these exercises. Additional blank outline maps can be found on the textbook's Web site: www.whfreeman.com/pulsipher5e.

1. Physical geography and population

The physical geography of Australia may play an important role in population distribution.

- On a blank map of Australia, using Figure 11.1 (regional map), delineate the interior deserts and basins with light yellow and label them. Then color the one principal river system in blue. Finally, color the eastern mountain ranges with brown.
- Using Photo Essay 11.1 (climate map), color the climate zones. Include an appropriate legend so that the zones can be identified.
- Draw a dot and label cities with populations of 1 million or greater, as depicted in Photo Essay 11.4 (population density map).

a. Make at least two generalizations about Australia's population concentrations based on physical geography characteristics.

b. Make at least two generalizations about Australia's population concentrations based on climatic zones.

c. What are some unique challenges faced by people inhabiting regions with low population densities?

d. What are some unique challenges faced by people inhabiting regions with high population densities?

2. The United Nations Convention on the Law of the Sea

The UN Convention on the Law of the Sea has particular impacts on this region.

* On a blank map of Oceania, approximate the 200-mile exclusive economic zone that each country can exploit. Draw this border around the island nations. You will have to make generalizations because of the scale at which you will be working.

Questions

a. The United Nations Convention on the Law of the Sea designates that countries sharing overlapping areas will draw a border midway between their coasts. Use a cross hatch marking (///) to identify any areas that may be in conflict. Suggest three possible conflicts that may arise.

b. Based on your understanding of Oceania, suggest benefits exclusive to these nations that are a result of the Law of the Sea Treaty.

c. Who do you think are the major global participants in exploiting the exclusive economic zones? How can small independent island nations be assertive in defining cooperation with those who want to "lease" these zones?

d. Compare the gains and losses discussed above and decide the overall value of the Law of the Sea Treaty to Oceania.

3. Global warming threatens Oceania

A single meter rise in the sea level can have profound impacts on some of the islands and countries in this region.

* Using a blank map of Oceania, color-code the islands according to their status of high island or low island. Refer to the CIA World Factbook at for information about elevation minimums and maximums (www.cia.gov/cia/publications/factbook).

Questions

a. Suggest at least two impacts that high islands will experience if global warming results in a one meter rise in ocean levels. Identify at least two impacts that the low islands will experience if global warming results in a one meter rise in ocean levels. These impacts may or may not be mutually exclusive.

b. Identify strategies that these islands should follow to prevent catastrophic effects from global warming. What strategies are specific to high islands? What strategies are specific to low islands?

SAMPLE EXAM QUESTIONS

The following are sample questions to help you review for an exam. Answers are found in the back of this study guide.

1.   Which of the following describes the climate changes typically associated with an El Niño event in the western Pacific (Oceania)?
a) Ocean temperatures *warm* up, which results in *more* cloud cover and rain.
b) Ocean temperatures *cool* down, which results in *less* cloud cover and rain.
c) Ocean temperatures *cool* down, which results in *more* cloud cover and rain.
d) Ocean temperatures *warm* up, which results in *less* cloud cover and rain.

2. Global warming in Oceania may or does result in all of the following except:
a) increased wildfires.
b) higher levels of human fertility.
c) coral bleaching.
d) stronger tropical storms.

3. Which of the following is not a common method of water management in Australia and New Zealand?
a) water harvesting from roofs
b) the build of dams
c) drip irrigation technologies
d) water-filtration techniques

4. Which of the following is the dominant land use in Australia, consuming more than 15 percent of all land?
a) plantation agriculture
b) mineral mining
c) transportation
d) cattle and sheep grazing

5. The name Melanesia comes from
a) the protective pigment found in the dark skin tones of its people.
b) European colonization practices.
c) a lost language of the indigenous people.
d) the name of the god thought to protect the region.

6. Since the 1960s and early 1970s, what world region has emerged as a significant market for the products of Oceania's countries, particularly Australia and New Zealand?
a) South America
b) Asia
c) Africa
d) Russia and Belarus

7. Why is the status of human well-being in the Pacific islands probably higher than statistics indicate?
a) The statistics do not take into account subsistence affluence and strong communitarian values.
b) The drug trade is off-the-books and introduces a lot of money to the economy.
c) Inherited wealth is handed down from generation to generation and does not appear as income.
d) Most education occurs in the home, so school attendance numbers do not indicate the correct overall level of education.

8. Which of the following describes the term *residential tourism*, which is a particularly important form of tourism in Hawaii?
a) observing people in their natural village settings
b) protecting the cultural aspects of one's local community against outsiders
c) relocating to warmer climates upon retirement
d) pseudonym for the sex trade

9. Which of the following statements provides the most accurate description of the composition of the populations of Australia and New Zealand since the 1990s?
a) Ethnic diversity is increasing.
b) The proportion of people of European descent is increasing.
c) The population of people claiming indigenous roots is declining.
d) The percentage of Asians is declining.

10. Which is the best description of the Pacific Way?
a) A political and cultural philosophy based on consensus and respect for traditional leadership.
b) A charity geared toward helping the poor and indigent of the Pacific islands.
c) The air currents that travel east to west around the globe at the "roaring forties."
d) The cross-country highway that unites Western Australia with Queensland and the Great Barrier Reef.

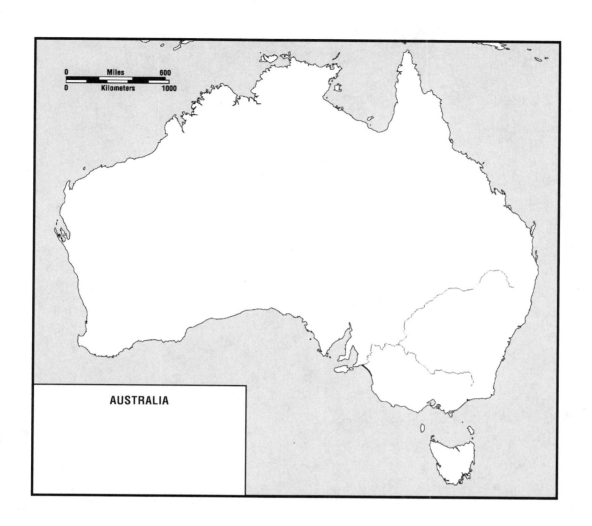

AUSTRALIA

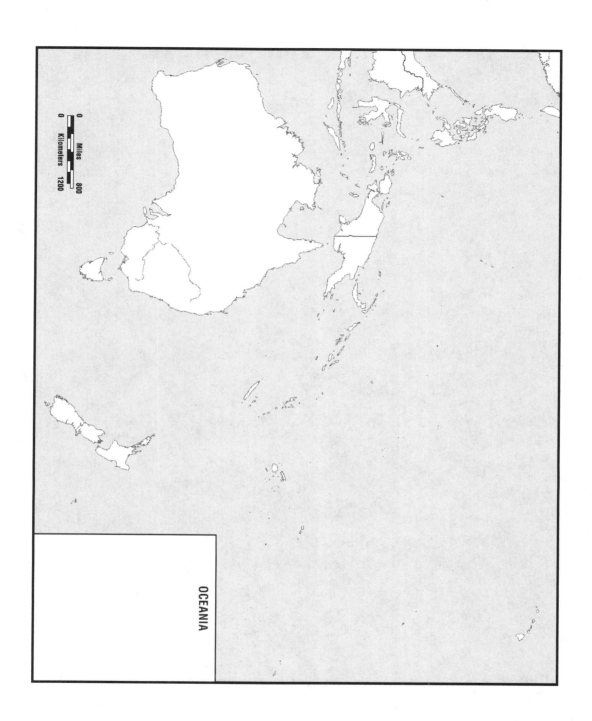

OCEANIA

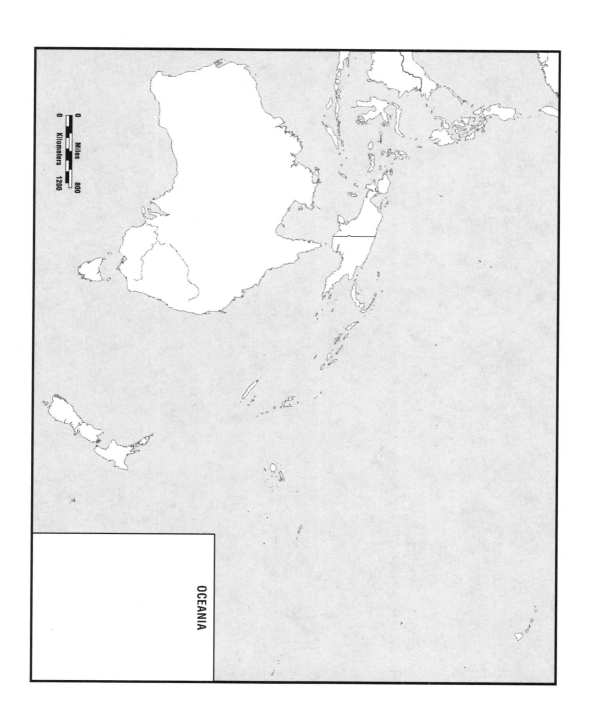

OCEANIA

APPENDIX A

ANSWERS TO SAMPLE EXAM QUESTIONS

Chapter 1

1. D
2. A
3. A
4. A
5. A
6. D
7. D
8. C
9. D
10. C

Chapter 2

1. B
2. B
3. C
4. A
5. A
6. B
7. C
8. B
9. B
10. B

Chapter 3

1. D
2. D
3. D
4. A
5. C
6. C
7. D
8. A
9. B
10. D

Chapter 4

1. B
2. B
3. C
4. C
5. D
6. C
7. C
8. A
9. B
10. B

Chapter 5

1. B
2. B
3. C
4. A
5. A
6. B
7. C
8. B
9. B
10. B

Chapter 6

1. D
2. B
3. D
4. A
5. A
6. C
7. C
8. A
9. A
10. A

Chapter 7

1. D
2. A
3. D
4. D
5. D
6. A
7. B
8. A
9. D
10. C

Chapter 8

1. B
2. D
3. B
4. A
5. D
6. C
7. B
8. C
9. D
10. D

Chapter 9

1. C
2. A
3. A
4. C
5. C
6. C
7. A
8. A
9. D
10. D

Chapter 10

1. B
2. C
3. A
4. C
5. B
6. B
7. C
8. A
9. D
10. A

Chapter 11

1. B
2. B
3. B
4. D
5. A
6. B
7. A
8. C
9. A
10. A

APPENDIX B

BLANK WORLD MAPS

Additional blank maps can be found at: www.whfreeman.com/pulsipher5e

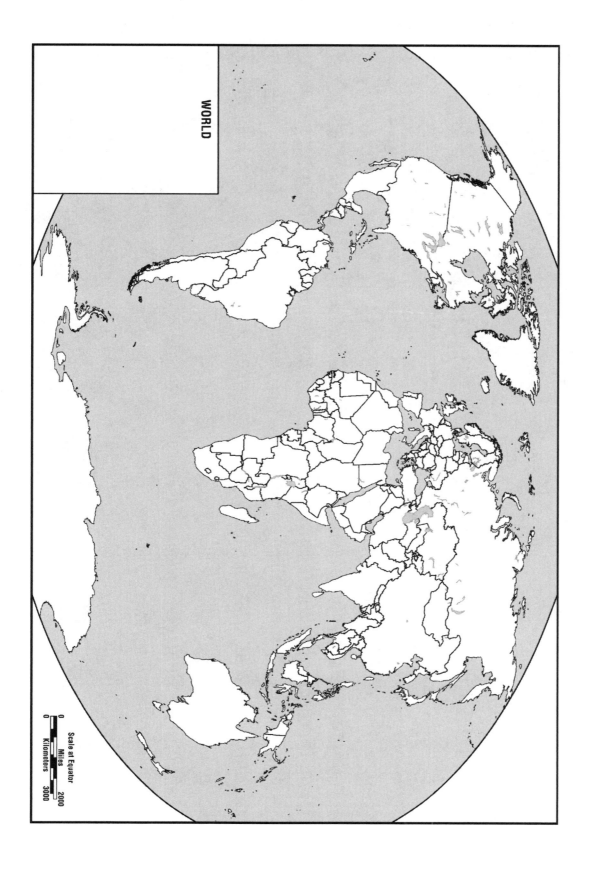

WORLD

Scale at Equator
Miles
0   2000
Kilometers
0   3000

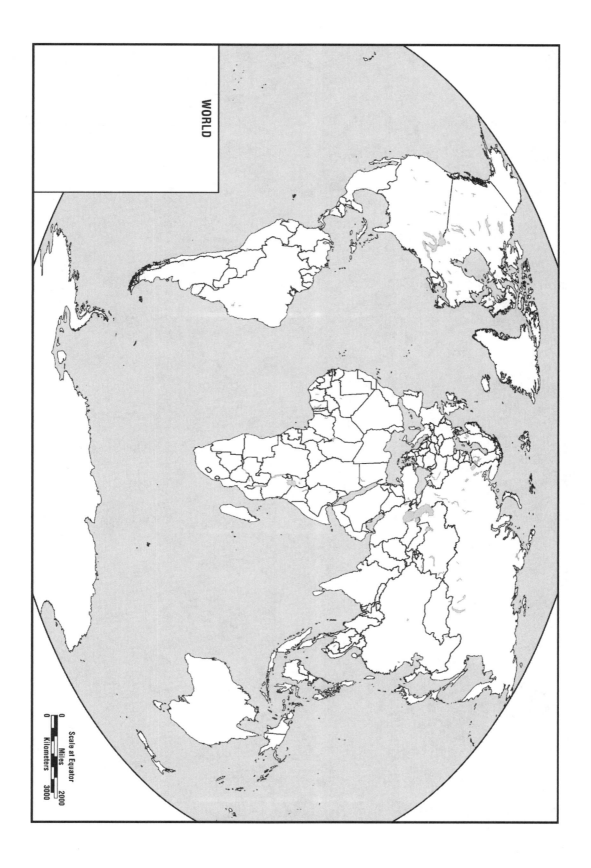

WORLD

Scale at Equator

Miles
0   2000

Kilometers
0   3000

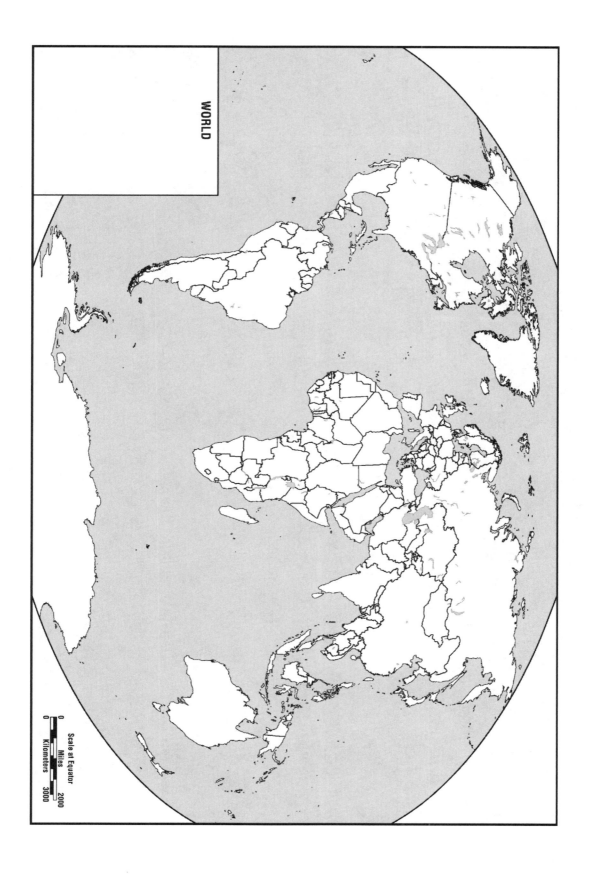

WORLD

Scale at Equator

0   2000
Miles

0   3000
Kilometers